Live an Eco-Friendly Life

52 **Brilliant Ideas**

one good idea can change your life

Live an
Eco-Friendly Life

Smart Ways to Get Green
and Stay That Way

Natalia Marshall

A Perigee Book

A PERIGEE BOOK
Published by the Penguin Group
Penguin Group (USA) Inc.
375 Hudson Street, New York, New York 10014, USA
Penguin Group (Canada), 90 Eglinton Avenue East, Suite 700, Toronto, Ontario M4P 2Y3, Canada
(a division of Pearson Penguin Canada Inc.)
Penguin Books Ltd., 80 Strand, London WC2R 0RL, England
Penguin Group Ireland, 25 St. Stephen's Green, Dublin 2, Ireland (a division of Penguin Books Ltd.)
Penguin Group (Australia), 250 Camberwell Road, Camberwell, Victoria 3124, Australia
(a division of Pearson Australia Group Pty. Ltd.)
Penguin Books India Pvt. Ltd., 11 Community Centre, Panchsheel Park, New Delhi—110 017, India
Penguin Group (NZ), 67 Apollo Drive, Rosedale, North Shore 0632, New Zealand
(a division of Pearson New Zealand Ltd.)
Penguin Books (South Africa) (Pty.) Ltd., 24 Sturdee Avenue, Rosebank, Johannesburg 2196, South Africa

Penguin Books Ltd., Registered Offices: 80 Strand, London WC2R 0RL, England

While the author has made every effort to provide accurate telephone numbers and Internet addresses at the time of publication, neither the publisher nor the author assumes any responsibility for errors, or for changes that occur after publication. Further, the publisher does not have any control over and does not assume any responsibility for author or third-party websites or their content.

LIVE AN ECO-FRIENDLY LIFE

First American edition: March 2008
Originally published as *Save the Planet* in Great Britain in 2007 by The Infinite Ideas Company Limited.

Perigee trade paperback ISBN: 978-0-399-53396-9

PRINTED IN THE UNITED STATES OF AMERICA

10   9   8   7   6   5   4   3   2   1

Most Perigee books are available at special quantity discounts for bulk purchases for sales promotions, premiums, fund-raising, or educational use. Special books, or book excerpts, can also be created to fit specific needs. For details, write: Special Markets, Penguin Group (USA) Inc., 375 Hudson Street, New York, New York 10014.

Brilliant ideas

Brilliant features

Each chapter of this book is designed to provide you with an inspirational idea that you can read quickly and put into practice right away.

Throughout you'll find four features that will help you get straight to the heart of the idea:

■ *Here's an idea for you* Take it on board and give it a try—right here, right now. Get an idea of how well you're doing so far.

■ *Try another idea* If this idea looks like a life-changer then there's no time to lose. *Try another idea* will point you straight to a related tip to enhance and expand on the first.

■ *Defining idea* Words of wisdom from masters and mistresses of the art, plus some interesting hangers-on.

■ *How did it go?* If at first you do succeed, try to hide your amazement. If, on the other hand, you don't, then this is where you'll find a Q and A that highlights common problems and how to get over them.

One small step...

Take a look at your watch: Within the next hour you could be doing your part to conserve the planet's precious resources, reduce pollution, and slow down climate change.

The news these days is full of stories about issues such as soaring carbon dioxide emissions, global warming, water shortages, toxins, and pollution. Few people now deny that our lifestyles are to blame, and that things have to change—sooner rather than later.

But it can seem very overwhelming. Where do I start? What can I do? Am I doing enough? These are probably some of the questions you've been asking.

The good news is that each and every one of us can take steps to make a difference, and ultimately make the world a better and healthier place. It may sometimes be tempting to blame faraway countries and politicians, but the fact of the matter is that we must all take some kind of responsibility.

And it is very easy to start making a difference; I've done it, and so can you. Even basic measures such as switching to energy-saving lightbulbs or starting a compost bin are a step in the right direction. I found using the mantra "reduce, reuse, and recycle" an invaluable building block. Stick to that, and you can't go wrong!

Once you've got your head around the basics, you'll be surprised how easy it is to go on to the next stage, and the next. Before you know where you are, you'll find yourself slyly patting your own back, secure in the knowledge you are well on your way to a greener, cleaner existence. If you take on just a fraction of the ideas I've suggested in this book, you'll be doing your part for a more sustainable future.

It can be uniquely satisfying to lead a simpler, less resource-hungry life, too. Research shows overwhelmingly that being part of a community (in this case, the eco gang!), appreciating the simple and natural, and acting positively greatly contribute toward personal happiness. And, what's more, many of the ideas in this book can help you save money.

So it's a win–win situation!

You certainly don't have to be living in an idyllic rural backwater to "go green," either. If, like me, you are an ordinary city dweller with a pretty hectic schedule, you can easily adapt your lifestyle so it is less wasteful and more thoughtful. One thing I have learned is that it takes no more time to live green than any other way. And if your home's in a city, you'll have handy access to all kinds of resources to help you on your way.

If you just do one idea in this book, that's a great start. Take up a few more, and you're well on your way.

Start with the small things that fit into your daily routine easily and work up to biggies when you feel comfortable. Bear in mind that doing something is better than doing nothing. Our own small actions as individuals add up to a huge global effort, and this is the only way that the planet can recover.

1

Saint or sinner?

The first step to a greener lifestyle is to take a long, hard look at your current one. Is the way you live trashing the planet or nurturing it?

Let's face it, we're not all as honest as we could be when it comes to assessing our lifestyles. So indulge in a little navel gazing, and take this lighthearted quiz as a starting point for change.

If, like me, you are full of good intentions but decidedly lacking in willpower, it helps to know your weak spots. We all buy too many things that waste precious resources, drive cars and travel on planes that produce CO_2 emissions, overheat and cool our homes artificially (which does the same thing), and pour toxic chemicals down the drain, which eventually end up in the sea.

Let's face it, as a generation we're spoiled rotten, and we may not even be fully aware of the detrimental effect our self-indulgent habits are having on poor old Earth. There's nothing like a bit of self-assessment to kick-start the conscience. The idea

Here's an idea for you...

Spend a day, or part of a day, with a notepad at your side (recycled paper, of course!), and jot down as many mundane activities as you can. Then try to divide them into two groups: "wasteful" or "not wasteful." If more than half of them are in the latter group then you can give yourself a pat on the back. If you find it tricky, don't worry—the simple action of writing things down will get you thinking about the way you live.

behind the quiz is to give you a rough idea of how much work you need to do in your quest for a greener lifestyle that leaves less of an imprint on our troubled planet.

1 **How do you mainly shop for food?**
   (a) You don't—it's all home-produced.
   (b) Online certified organic delivery services.
   (c) At local markets and groceries.
   (d) At the supermarket.
2 **It's lunchtime in the office. Do you:**
   (a) Dive into your organic, homemade packed lunch?
   (b) Order something decent at an upmarket macrobiotic café?
   (c) Go where everyone else is going, e.g., the bar?
   (d) Head for the nearest fast-food chain or work cafeteria?
3 **How do you get to work/school?**
   (a) Walk or cycle.
   (b) Take public transportation.
   (c) Carpool.
   (d) Drive.

Defining idea...

"Everyone thinks of changing the world, but no one thinks of changing himself."

TOLSTOY

4 **When the temperature drops, what do you do?**
   (a) Do nothing—your home is insulated and solar-powered.
   (b) Put on another jacket and shiver.
   (c) Turn up the thermostat just a little.
   (d) Crank up the heating as far as it goes and bring in extra heaters.

5 **What kind of vacations do you usually take?**
   (a) A working conservation holiday.
   (b) Something low-key and national.
   (c) A package vacation somewhere warm.
   (d) As exotic and far-flung as possible.

6 **What are your cleaning materials of choice?**
   (a) Lemon juice and baking soda.
   (b) Eco-friendly products.
   (c) Anything from the supermarket that works.
   (d) A whole army of brand-name cleaners, sprays, wipes, and liquids.

7 **How much do you recycle?**
   (a) Virtually everything, and the rest goes to charity.
   (b) Newspapers, bottles, cans, vegetable matter.
   (c) Newspapers and maybe bottles sometimes.
   (d) Nothing—it all goes straight in the trash.

8 **What kind of car do you own?**
   (a) You don't.
   (b) A small, low-emission model.
   (c) A minivan or family sedan.
   (d) A nice big SUV.

If you suspect your home is not quite as green as it could be, read IDEA 3, *Clarity begins at home*, for a few tips on cutting your carbon footprint.

Try another idea...

"Never doubt that a small group of thoughtful, committed citizens can change the world; indeed, it is the only thing that ever has."
MARGARET MEAD

Defining idea...

3

9 **What sort of presents did you give last Christmas/birthday?**
   (a) You didn't—the money went straight to charity instead.
   (b) Ethical presents for good causes.
   (c) Catalog/online goods where some profits go to charity.
   (d) Whatever the recipients wanted.

10 **How ethical is your bank?**
   (a) Very. That's why you chose it.
   (b) It has several good environmental policies.
   (c) Not sure, but hopefully pretty good.
   (d) You went for the best deal—ethics didn't come into it.

Mainly a's. Congratulations, you are fully committed to the environment and well on your way to becoming a green goddess—or god, of course.

Mainly b's. You're definitely aware of what it takes to be green although there are one or two luxuries you're not prepared to give up just yet. But keep up the good work, and you'll be doing your part for the planet in no time.

Mainly c's. The will to change is there, but you've got a way to go before you win the Zayed Prize for the Environment. You just need to spend a little more time thinking about how your actions could affect the planet.

Defining idea…

"You must be the change you wish to see in the world."
MAHATMA GANDHI

Mainly d's. Oh dear, you're something of a walking eco-disaster. Time to change your wasteful and spendthrift habits for a greener, cleaner lifestyle.

Q **How long will it take me to go from a sinful D-grader to a straight-A star?**

How did it go?

A *You can't change your entire life in a day, and nobody would expect you to. But the beauty of learning to live in a more sustainable way is that you can start with seemingly tiny changes and build up from there. After all, if the six billion people on this earth all picked up one piece of litter, imagine how much cleaner it would be. Think of it as personal evolution!*

Q **How can I decide whether something I do is "wasteful" or not?**

A *I suppose you could argue that anything we do is wasteful, from breathing in air to wearing out the pavements walking! But being sensible, you could try asking yourself a few questions: Does the action produce pollution; does it produce waste material; and does it use up resources? If the answer is yes to more than one, classify it as wasteful.*

Q **I'd like to be more environmentally aware. How can I measure my progress?**

A *Why not start an eco-diary? Make it weekly, if you like, or even monthly. At the end of each week or month you could write down what changes you have made. You could also include how the changes make you feel, and the impact on your family, personal, or professional life. It will make interesting reading later on!*

2

Hey, big spender

You're revving up to do your part for the planet, right? You may have to give up some luxuries along the way, but the fact that going greener will boost your happiness levels should more than compensate.

The study of happiness is a new science, but one or two "happy factors" come up time and again when the experts tell us about the path to enlightenment. And, you've guessed it, tuning into the environment is one of them!

Do you ever feel overwhelmed by excessive choice? It's a twenty-first-century thing, and it can seriously damage your happiness. Call it the satisfaction treadmill: The more options we have, the more we think that there is a perfect choice out there. (Cell phones are a good example of this!) The pressure is on to find perfection, and yet that perfect choice eludes us, so it's back to square one. Think of kids in a candy store …

Living more sustainably means letting go of some creature comforts. That's not to say you have to go all spartan and austere. It's just about being a little more thought-

Here's an idea for you...

Is your home chock-full of "useful" gadgets? Why not make a hit list of all the electric "labor-saving" devices you own. I'm not talking major appliances here, but gadgets like electric milk frothers, cheese graters, can openers, massage wands, mini-fans, popcorn makers, pepper grinders, and the like. They all use up valuable resources—what's wrong with some elbow power? And, while you're in decluttering mode, pack them up and send them to a secondhand shop or recycle them. It's all too easy to buy something you don't need because of the hype surrounding it. One of the starting blocks of eco-living is refusing to be overwhelmed by consumer choice, and only buying what you really need.

Defining idea...

"Excess choice leads to unfreedom."

DR. BARRY SCHWARTZ,
psychology professor

ful, and perhaps accepting that we can't all have everything all of the time. In time, leading a less frantic, less cluttered existence should bring immense satisfaction to you and others around you.

After all, the things that bring us happiness don't just come in a package, bottle, or bag. Far from it: Research shows that the old cliché "the best things in life are free" is absolutely true!

Start by taking a look at the way we live today. In the Western, developed world, standards of living, health care, welfare, and education have improved hugely in the last century or so. Many of us have two cars or more, our houses are full of electrical goodies, we vacation more often, eat well, and have generally thrown ourselves heart and soul into the consumer party.

Yet research carried out in the US and Europe has shown that our contentment levels haven't really increased since the 1950s. Seems like that old adage has been scientifically proven: Money can't buy you happiness. The gladness gurus have found there's a global minimum living standard that equalizes everyone, and after that it doesn't much matter whether you're a billionaire or a bus driver.

It follows, then, that ditching some of your consumer goodies won't make you any less happy; in fact the opposite could be true. Leading a greener lifestyle certainly involves material sacrifices, but there are tons of compensations that should have you feeling like a million dollars.

If the thought of doing something for others strikes a chord with you, why not try volunteering? There are lots of opportunities out there, so read up about them in IDEA 47, *Get involved*.

Try another idea...

Try this exercise, which picks up on some of the proven happy factors pinpointed by happiness psychologists.

Think back over your life and jot down the half a dozen or so happy times you can remember. Then, see how many of them tie in with one of the categories below:

1   Finding a meaning in life; for instance, religion, spirituality, or philosophy. (Or caring for the planet!)
2   Setting/achieving active goals, ideally ones that use our strengths and abilities.
3   Belonging to a community.
4   Spending time in the natural environment.
5   Getting involved with social issues.
6   Volunteering/helping others.

All of the above fit in beautifully with more eco-friendly living, so crack open the organic, carbon-free champagne, and look forward to your new, green lifestyle.

"Sometimes it falls upon a generation to be great. You can be that great generation. Let your greatness blossom."
NELSON MANDELA

Defining idea...

How did it go?

Q   Will leading a simpler, greener life really make me happier?

A   *If you think of a time when you've been pretty happy, chances are it was when you were busy doing something useful, had a good network of relationships, or were learning a new skill rather than a time when you had loads of money or a new car. Now you can add "being green" to the list! You should start feeling the benefits of a greener lifestyle at once, and this will build as you achieve more eco-goals.*

Q   My possessions represent years of hard work. Do I have to ditch them all and start living like a monk?

A   *Of course not. It's more a question of evaluating what you have, and thinking more carefully about what you buy next time. You can learn to say no, too—whether it's to pestering from the kids or to well-meaning friends who insist on buying costly birthday presents. We've all been there.*

Q   What difference will it make to the planet if I simply cut back on gadgets?

A   *Quite a lot in the long run, as it means reducing the amount of electricity and manufacturing resources you use. Each and every individual can make a difference, no matter how small. It's also a question of critical mass, getting to the point where, if you're not doing it, you are the one who's left out! Think how much more socially acceptable smoking and not wearing a seat belt used to be, for instance.*

3

Clarity begins at home

"Carbon footprint" is the buzzword when it comes to living greener. We all have one, and the fastest way to reduce it is to make your home a greener place.

Your home is probably your main source of pollution. Hard to accept, isn't it? But once you turn eco-spy, you'll find ways of making it green.

Everyone's heard the saying "think global, act local." Well, your own home is about as local as it gets. And the way you live at home can have worldwide implications.

Let's start with the all-important carbon footprint that everyone's talking about at the moment. The main thing about it is, we don't want one! Or at least, we want a small one, so in this case, size does matter.

Your carbon footprint is the imprint your activities leave on the environment in terms of the amount of greenhouse gases produced, measured in units of carbon dioxide. Everything you do at home, from the way you dispose of waste to the temperature on your thermostat, has an impact on the size of your carbon footprint.

Here's an idea for you...

It's quite an undertaking to turn your home eco-friendly. If it seems a bit daunting, why not carry out a mini audit one room at a time? Start with the smallest room in the house—the bathroom! Every detail counts: Is the toilet paper roll recycled paper, are the lightbulbs energy savers, are the cleaning materials toxic, how much water is flushed, is the tap water overheated, and even is the toilet seat made from forest friendly wood from a certified source? It all has an impact. And from there, you can progress to the rest of the house.

Defining idea...

"A lot of people doing a little bit really is effective."

DR. CHRIS WEST, climate expert

And man-made CO_2 is one of the biggest contributors to global warming. The net result of this climate change is sadly not going to be lovely hot summers and pleasant, mild winters. Instead, glaciers and sea ice will melt, sea levels will rise, and coastal areas will flood. Inland areas will become hotter and drier, and lakes and rivers could dry up. There will be more droughts, making it hard to grow crops, and some plants and animals might become extinct because of the heat. Hurricanes, tornadoes, and other storms may get more common.

Overall, the cost to society, the environment, our health, and the economy is likely to far outweigh any benefits.

But we can all help contain global warming, starting with minimizing your footprint— and there's no time like the present. We'll be looking at ways of reducing your carbon footprint throughout this book, but there are things you can do today, in your home, to reduce your contribution to global warming. Best of all, they should not cost you a penny, and in the long term will save you cash.

- Sign up for greener energy.
- Turn down the central and water heating slightly.
- Use dishwashers, washing machines, and driers at full capacity, or use half-load programs.
- Don't leave appliances on standby.
- Hang the laundry out to dry rather than tumble drying.
- Install energy-saving lightbulbs.
- Insulate your hot water tank, your attic, and your walls.
- Recycle and reuse.
- Save water by harvesting rainwater, reusing "gray" water, and cutting down on watering.

Save cash as well as energy by following some of the tips in IDEA 13, *Warm and cozy*. Your carbon footprint will thank you for it!

Try another idea...

Apart from global warming, general pollution threatens our health, crops, and wildife. You can help reduce pollution with all of the above steps. As a bonus, you could also switch to organic food and use fewer chemicals around the home.

Once you've got the ball rolling, make sure your whole household is involved. Get teenagers to switch off gadgets and lights when not in use; explain to the kids how recycling works and ask them to help you sort your trash into the right bins; persuade Granny to share her make-do-and-mend tips and Granddad his compost recipe. Encourage the whole family to cut back on water usage, for instance by not leaving taps running; and get everyone used to having the house slightly cooler. And just watch your carbon footprint shrink!

"We forget that the water cycle and the life cycle are one."

JACQUES-YVES COUSTEAU

Defining idea...

13

How did it go?

Q   Can I really make a difference just by turning off appliances?

A   It's as simple as that. Electricity is one of the biggest producers of carbon emissions, so every time you make coffee or turn the television on you are adding to global warming. Up to a third of carbon dioxide emissions are caused by the domestic sector—that's you and me—so every household has its part to play. For example, if every household in the United States installed one energy-saving bulb, the energy saved could power a city of 1.5 million.

Q   I love the idea of being greener but how can I move things forward?

A   Don't think you have to kick off your new lifestyle by swapping your fan heater for a wind turbine! Start with the small, manageable stuff such as recycling, turning off appliances, and saving water. If it helps, why not draw up a plan of action, with steps you can take today, next week, and next year?

Q   Will I have to reduce my standard of living if I carry out some of the ideas you suggest?

A   Not at all. It's more a question of swapping one kind of good lifestyle for another. It's always a challenge making changes and sticking to them, especially when you can't always see the immediate effect. But think of it as switching to a low-fat diet: The effects are holistic and will be visible over time.

4

Once more with feeling

There really isn't any excuse not to recycle. It's easier than ever, and almost the entire contents of your wastebasket can have a second, or even third, life.

I know people who still throw almost all their trash away, and I always flinch when I see it. Is it so hard to simply separate waste materials and put the good stuff into different containers?

You wouldn't store fresh and frozen food together, keep the toys in with the cutlery, or wash lights and darks together, would you?

Or at least, I hope not. So you are already familiar with the principle of sorting. And recycling works in very much the same way: You sort your waste into three or four different categories, and then pass it on to be used again.

It really couldn't be simpler. Local authorities across the world are falling over themselves to encourage us to recycle with curbside collections; recycling centers

Here's an idea for you... **If you're not quite wedded to the idea of recycling yet, why not try it for one week? In just seven days you will be astonished (and possibly horrified) to see a small mountain of recyclable newspapers, food packaging, bottles, vegetable peelings, and lawn cuttings build up. Recycle and your usual trash bags will shrink to almost nothing!**

here, there, and everywhere; and civic amenity sites where you can send everything from aerosols to zinc to be reused. In many countries, individual households recycle at least 60 percent of their waste and there's no reason why everyone can't aim for this, or even more.

The great thing about recycling is that the effects are immediate. Just think: Your old CDs could be made into designer clocks, coasters, or even calendars. Unwanted cell phones can be reconditioned and donated to charity. Soda cans can be recycled and the money raised used to plant more trees. Plastic bottles can be converted into fleeces and garden furniture. What could be better than knowing that your unwanted junk can genuinely be put to good use? And it declutters at the same time! Even the smallest change in the way we approach the disposal of our waste would make a big difference if universally adopted.

Recycling helps in many ways: We send less trash to the landfill or incineration, and we save valuable materials and energy. For example, recycling aluminium cans saves 95 percent of the energy used in making a new can.

Defining idea... *"Garbage is the waste of a throwaway society— ecological societies have never had garbage."*
DR. VANDANA SHIVA, campaigner

The other great thing is that recycling doesn't cost you a penny, and as you become more aware of the amount of waste you generate, you may even become a more efficient homeowner along the way.

THE THREE R'S–REDUCE, REUSE, RECYCLE

We would all benefit from:

- Reducing the amount of trash we create;
- Reusing stuff we normally throw away; and
- Recycling more.

Reduce

If you opt to buy only the right quantity of what you need, you're not being cheap—just eco-savvy.

- Choose products with less packaging and buy secondhand where you can.
- Buy more fresh produce or grow your own. This uses less packaging and it's healthy, too!
- Reduce paper and ink waste by printing out only what you need, condensing text, reducing print quality, and using both sides of the paper.
- Store food in resealable containers instead of plastic wrap or tinfoil.
- Use rechargeable batteries: Although pricier, they will reduce waste and save you money in the long run.
- Register with the Mail Preference Service to stop getting junk mail.

Reuse

Cut down on the amount of trash you generate by reusing materials.

Set aside your fruit and veggie scraps for the compost bin. Find out how to make the perfect garden fertilizer in IDEA 33, *Lovely, leafy compost.*

Try another idea...

"Use it up, wear it out, make it do, or do without."
NEW ENGLAND PROVERB

Defining idea...

- Repair broken appliances and shoes or donate them to charity to delay the point where they become waste.
- Reuse plastic bags (or better still, buy a durable shopping bag).
- Keep scrap paper for telephone messages/lists, etc.
- Try to buy products such as milk or cosmetics that come in refillable packaging. Some specialist retailers, such as The Body Shop, offer this refill service, as do some delivery services.
- Keep worn-out clothing, towels, or bed linens to use as household cleaning cloths.
- Spruce up old furniture rather than throwing it out.
- Choose reusable products over disposable: sponges rather than wipes, tea towels rather than paper towels. Opt for cloth diapers, but wash them with an eco-product at a lowish temperature and hang them out rather than tumble dry them.

Recycle

Find out about your neighborhood's facilities and get going. Recyclable items include: aerosols, batteries, drink cartons, cans, paper and cardboard, plastic bags/bottles, CDs, ink cartridges, computers, some furniture, metal, glass, electrical goods, paint, clothes, textiles, shoes, and food packaging.

Other things like toys, household items, bikes, books, bricks, and rubble can be sold or given to charity.

- Keep separate bins in your house so that you can separate recyclable waste as soon as it's ready.
- Start a compost heap. It's simple, cheap, and will provide you with free natural fertilizer.

- Buy products made from recycled materials whenever possible.
- Find out which labels on packaging mean it can be recycled.

Q   **I'm new to the area and don't have a clue about the recycling facilities here. Where do I start?**

How did it go?

A   *Get in touch with your local government via phone, website, or in person. All cities and towns have a recycling policy, and should be able to tell you where and how you can help. You'll find it's easier than you think!*

Q   **How can I sort my waste so that it goes to the right place?**

A   *If your city or town doesn't provide door-to-door collection, why not start by bagging up newspapers, bottles, and cans that can then easily be taken to a local recycling center? Once you've got the hang of that, you can move onto other waste such as food packaging, plastic bottles and bags, and batteries, or raw vegetable matter that can be composted at home. You'll find it strangely addictive...*

Q   **How do I know whether something can be recycled or not?**

A   *Again, your local government should be able to help, and it does vary. But if you're not sure about something, start getting label savvy. More and more packaging is carrying some kind of logo, which should tell you whether it's recyclable or not.*

5

Detox your home

"Sick building syndrome" is a term often used to describe offices, but where you live can be just as unhealthy as where you work. Here's how to make your home a healthier and greener place.

Do you live in a closed box? Our hermetically sealed homes may reduce energy waste but they can also cause a buildup of toxins. Open a window occasionally to let the fresh air in and the bad stuff out.

It's a sad fact that most of us spend around 90 percent of our time indoors: at home, at school or work, and traveling in cars or public transportation. Windows tend to stay closed except for during the hottest weather, so unless you want to swap your home for a well-ventilated tent, you may be living in a toxic time bomb.

Some of the worst culprits for sick building syndrome are chemicals called Volatile Organic Compounds or VOCs, gases that are given off by many household items. You can't see them but you can sniff them—the fresh, plasticky smell of new carpet is one example.

Here's an idea for you...

The easiest and cheapest way to start detoxing your home is simply to open windows more. You don't need to freeze in gale force winds, but ten minutes of fresh air a day will let toxins out and fresh air in. It cuts down on the need for air fresheners, too.

These are the bad guys, and what's more, they are everywhere: floor coverings, furnishings, cleaning products, polishes, paints, plastics, air fresheners, pesticides, and aerosol sprays. VOCs can irritate skin, eyes, nose, and throat, and cause dizziness, nausea, and headaches.

The jury is still out on whether some of these chemicals cause more serious illnesses such as asthma, allergies, and cancer, but evidence seems to be building up. And babies and young children are certainly at greater risk from chemical exposures, which could affect their health and ability to learn.

Just as importantly, whatever goes down the drain or into the atmosphere eventually ends up in the ocean or back on the planet as rain. And all those toxins can eventually have a pretty big impact on the habitats of wildlife. Ingredients like phosphates, ammonia, and bleach have the potential to disrupt rivers, lakes, and ultimately oceans across the globe.

The best thing is obviously to cut back on chemicals in the home. Help reduce the toxic burden of manufacturing, your home, and the waste stream by choosing cleaners, cosmetics, and household products that are based on relatively harmless fruit acids and salts and are biodegradable. Use natural alternatives to pesticides. Switch to organic food where possible. Cut back on the amount of plastic in your home.

Defining idea...

"Water and air, the two essential fluids on which all life depends, have become global garbage cans."
JACQUES-YVES COUSTEAU

Avoid treated materials used in carpets, furniture covers, and cushions. Where possible, choose natural materials such as wool carpets, felt underlays, hemp, cotton, linen, wool, or hessian fabrics, and latex (rubber) or natural fiber cushions. Floor coverings and furnishings should be aired and cleaned regularly. Choose low maintenance, easy to clean floorings that can help prevent the buildup of dust and chemicals.

Our homes are full of potentially harmful chemicals. Find out more about how to root them out in IDEA 10, *Always read the label.*

Try another idea...

The cheapest and easiest way to improve the air inside is to let more of the outside air in. Air circulation dilutes pollutants and helps to keep mold at bay. Ensure there is good airflow through windows, doors, wall vents, and ducts. Plants are nature's air cleaners and having them inside can help to keep pollutants down.

Put computers, faxes, and copiers in a downstairs, well-ventilated room, but keep them away from bedrooms as the circuitry and inks emit volatile carbon toxins.

Check for carbon monoxide: Get flues and chimneys swept at least once a year, have all gas and solid fuel fires serviced regularly, don't sleep in unvented rooms with gas or kerosene heaters, and don't run cars, lawn mowers, or barbecues in the confines of the garage. Faulty or unflued gas appliances are major emitters of indoor air pollutants including carbon monoxide, nitrogen dioxide, air toxics, and particulates.

If you live in an old house, check for lead in paint and water pipes—ask your local environmental health officer for more information if you're worried.

"We do not inherit the earth from our ancestors; we borrow it from our children."
NAVAJO PROVERB

Defining idea...

23

How did it go?

Q **I'm getting older now and doubt that detoxing my home will have much effect on me. Is there any point in doing all the things you suggest?**

A *I should say so! Even if you think you are not personally affected, your children, grandchildren, and whoever next lives in your house may be affected. Besides, any steps you take benefit the environment as a whole.*

Q **I'd like my home to be "greener" but my partner thinks it's all a waste of time. How can I convince him?**

A *Stealth is usually as good a way as any! Start with the small steps such as bringing in more plants or switching to eco-products and organic food. These may cost a little more, but you can offset this by shopping more thoughtfully, cutting back on pricey disposable products and prepared meals, for instance. From there, move onto the bigger stuff. He'll soon start to notice the effects on his well-being and will be much more interested in helping you.*

Q **You're suggesting opening windows more, but doesn't that mean all the heat in the room will disappear? Aren't we all supposed to be conserving energy?**

A *Nobody's saying that you must keep all your windows open all of the time. Obviously this simply isn't practical. But keeping them open for ten minutes or so every day will clean the air a bit. Choose a time when the heating is at its lowest, perhaps at night or when the house tends to be emptiest.*

6

Clean but green

It's easy to get hooked on the latest domestic products that promise a life of ease and cleanliness, but do you really need them?

Whether you squirt, spray, foam, or wipe, commercial cleaners mean you're adding to the chemical imprint on your home and the environment.

I used to know an elderly lady who kept her coffee cups pristine white with high-strength household bleach. She did, in fact, live to a ripe old age, but I never felt happy about her cleaning methods and what effect they might be having on her health!

These days there is probably a special coffee cup whitener on the market—there is an insatiable demand for "special" cleaning products. But as fast as these come onto the supermarket shelves, more potentially harmful chemicals appear with them.

It's estimated that fewer than a quarter of the chemicals used in cleaning products have been subjected to a full safety investigation, while others, officially classified as hazardous, are still found as key ingredients.

Here's an idea for you...

Make your own household cleaner from less harmful ingredients, which you can buy in department stores and hardware shops or even online from eco-suppliers. Mix one teaspoon washing soda, four teaspoons borax, and one teaspoon liquid soap or detergent with four cups of hot water in a lidded plastic bottle or old spray container. Shake well to blend and dissolve the minerals. Spray the cleaner onto the surface you're cleaning or apply it with a cloth, wiping it off with a rag as you go. For tougher dirt, leave the mix on for a few minutes before removing. Shake the bottle each time before using. To save time, money, and packaging, make your cleaner in advance and buy the ingredients in bulk. Experiment to find a blend that suits you, and maybe add your favorite essential oils or herbs for fragrance.

The overuse of chemical cleaners has also given rise to the so-called hygiene hypothesis: Sanitation means less exposure to microbes, equals more asthma, allergic disease, and multiple sclerosis. Think of the immune system as a noisy, rowdy party, with plenty of bouncers to chuck out unwanted guests. Imagine that if there were no guests the bouncers might turn on each other, which is what happens in these kinds of autoimmune diseases.

We don't need to lead a sanitized, germ-free life; we need to be an integrated part of the ecosystem, not eradicate it from our homes!

SOFTLY, SOFTLY

Try some of these alternative—and kinder—cleaning materials.

- Soda crystals (sodium carbonate), also known as washing soda, used to be the most common household cleaning product. You can use soda crystals for kitchen floors, work surfaces, to clean the draining board and wall tiles, and, left overnight in the sink, they will clear stains.

- Bicarbonate of soda (baking soda) is also a good cleaner, and if you mix it with water you'll get an alkaline solution that dissolves dirt and grease. Use it dry to lift stains from carpets and marks from surfaces.

- Borax is a naturally occurring mineral, soluble in water. It can deodorize, remove mildew and mold, boost the cleaning power of soap or detergent, and remove stains.

- Corn flour can be used to clean windows, polish furniture, shampoo carpets and rugs, and starch clothes.

- Microfiber cloths are made with extra-long fibers that attract dust and remove dirt, cutting down on the need for chemical cleaners.

- Olive oil can be used sparingly as furniture polish.

- Soap flakes are good for clothes washing and as a general cleaner. Look out for flakes made from natural ingredients that will biodegrade.

- Sunlight is a useful, free bleach for household linen and all whites.

- Tea tree oil is a strong antiseptic and disinfectant that works on mold and mildew.

- White wine vinegar has many uses. It's a surface cleaner, stain remover, lime-scale descaler; it cuts through grease, deodorizes, and acts as a mild disinfectant. Use a half vinegar, half water solution to clean windows, tiles, and mirrors.

- Lemon juice is good for cleaning chopping boards and wooden surfaces, and can also act as a descaler. Lemon oil makes a good furniture polish.

There are low chemical and low energy ways to keep your wardrobe pristine, too—see IDEA 21, *Clothes care*.

Try another idea...

"Man does not live by soap alone."

GILBERT K. CHESTERTON

Defining idea...

How did it go?

Q   **I'm a complete hygiene nut. How effective are these natural cleaners?**

A   *Very, although some of them may work a little more slowly than chemical cleaners since by their nature they are gentler. (You have to ask yourself what on earth must be in some commercial cleaners that they remove dirt instantly!) If you're in a rush, you may be better off applying the cleaner, leaving it for a while to take effect while you do something else, and then rinsing it off later on. It may just take you a little while to get used to a slightly different approach to household chores.*

Q   **Are natural cleaners completely safe around children?**

A   *The cleaners mentioned here are a lot less dangerous than most chemical alternatives, but that doesn't mean you can leave them lying around where a child may take it into his head to have a swig from the bottle. It's best to make sure that any container with cleaners in it is clearly labeled with all ingredients and kept out of reach.*

Q   **I'm incredibly busy—will I have time to mix up potions rather than simply squirting ready-made cleaners around?**

A   *You can save time by making your cleaners in advance, buying the ingredients in bulk for cost savings and to avoid excess packaging. Make large batches of the recipes and store them in labeled, reusable airtight plastic containers and spray bottles.*

7

Kiss pests goodbye

We all have unwanted bugs and critters in our homes but there's no need to zap them with harmful pesticides when gentler, safer alternatives work just as well.

Six-legged guests such as moths, ants, and mosquitoes plague us all from time to time but they are still part of the ecosystem.

If insects and rodents make your skin crawl, it's sometimes hard to be kind to them! But it's worth overcoming your dislike when you realize that they have a role to play in the natural world, breaking down and recycling plant material, keeping the soil healthy, and providing food for other animals.

So treat them with respect and shoo them off rather than exterminate them. Using natural deterrents means you'll be helping to maintain the balance of the ecosystem and reducing your use of toxic pesticides.

MOTHS

It's understandably annoying when moths decide to snack on your favorite skirt or jacket. But spare a thought for the little fellas. Moths and their caterpillars are an important link in the food chain, providing a meal for many mammals, especially

Certain essential oils extracted from plants that smell delightful to us are highly effective at deterring bugs. They have lots of other uses, too, from first aid to natural air freshener or bath oil so you don't need to restrict their use to the summer months. Shop around for a good supplier and start to build up a small collection that includes pure tea tree, neem, rosemary, lavender, eucalyptus, cedar, and rose geranium. Keep them in a cool, dark place and they will last for months. They can be burned in a water burner, soaked into cotton balls, or, in some cases, diluted and applied sparingly to the skin (but read the label before applying).

bats and birds. Bear in mind, too, that mothballs are normally made of paradichlorobenzene, which is harmful to liver and kidneys. Aromatic cedar chips in a cheesecloth square, or cedar oil in an absorbent cloth, will repel moths. Homemade moth-repelling sachets can also be made with lavender, rosemary, vetiver, and rose petals.

ANTS

Ants dislike cayenne pepper, citrus oil (can be soaked into cotton balls), lemon juice, cloves, cinnamon or coffee grounds, fresh garlic, or dry crushed mint leaves. Keep counters free of crumbs and sticky spots, cover the sugar, and put the honey jar away. Cut off water sources such as drips or dishes left soaking overnight. But if ants still insist on invading your territory, keep a small spray bottle handy and spray the ants with soapy water.

DUST MITES

Microscopic dust mites are everywhere in the home—in our beds, clothing, furniture, and soft toys—even on our bookshelves! For people with allergies or asthma, dust mites are a problem, and they especially enjoy warm, moist conditions.

Wash sheets, pillows, and rugs in soapy water or borax, and use borax to clean hard surfaces, as it is a effective solution to the problem of dust mites.

Tannic acid, usually extracted from sumac bark or oak galls, is an important ingredient in the tanning of leather, and is also used to prevent allergenic outbreaks caused by dust mites. A solution of 3 percent tannic acid neutralizes the protein in dust mite fecal matter that causes most allergic reactions. Mix with water and spray the affected area; tannic acid can also be bought in dustable powder form, or you could even use a very strong solution of tea!

Rosemary oil is also good; it kills mites by drying out the moisture that they need. Wipe down surfaces with a few drops added to water, or add to the laundry rinse.

If creepy crawlies and other outdoor pests are proving less than welcome in the garden, find out natural ways of getting rid of them in IDEA 36, *Your very own mini eco-park.*

Try another idea...

MOSQUITOES

Effective bug repellents include oil of eucalyptus and one part garlic juice with five parts water in a small spray bottle. Strips of cotton cloth can also be dipped in this mixture and hung in areas, such as patios, as a localized deterrent.

Neem oil is a safe, natural vegetable oil that contains sallanin, a compound that has effective mosquito repelling properties. Citronella oil is said to be good, too.

"If insects disappeared, the world would collapse within weeks."

DAVID ATTENBOROUGH

Defining idea...

HEAD LICE

These pesky visitors invade most children's scalps at some time or other and are becoming increasingly immune to commercial lotions. The best way of getting rid of them is by wet combing with a nit comb. After washing the hair add a few drops of lice-repellent essential oil through the hair. The best oils are neem, rosemary, lavender, eucalyptus, and rose geranium, which can also be added to shampoo.

FLIES

Fly sprays often contain toxic gases and chemicals that don't do your health any favors and also kill bees and can harm and kill aquatic life when their residues enter water systems. Try natural deterrents instead such as lemon, cloves, pine, and cedar oils. Nontoxic fly paper based on natural ingredients works well, too. (Yes, I know they look awful, but they make good nontoxic solutions!)

Q **Is it true that citronella is a good natural insect repellent?**

How did it go?

A *Citronella, which is made from lemongrass, is a very popular bug buster, and has been available in candle, spray, soap, and crystal form. There is some doubt about its efficacy. However, many people, especially horse owners, swear by it, and make up their own sprays as citronella itself is widely available.*

Q **How can I keep my home free of ants and flies?**

A *It's always best to remove the source of whatever it is that attracts them. Food left lying around, surface dirt, sources of still water, e.g., birdbaths, rotten wood, and warm, moist conditions all tend to be big attractors, so tackle these areas first.*

8

You've got the power

The electricity that powers our homes can be produced by a number of different sources. Have you ever thought about where yours comes from?

All utility services are definitely not equal—some are much greener than others!

If every time you switch on a light you feel a pang of guilt, now might be the time to switch your electricity to a "green" supplier.

When electricity is manufactured conventionally, it produces emissions such as sulphur dioxide and carbon dioxide. These pollutants not only add to global warming but also contribute to acid rain. Electricity produced using renewable energy produces far less environmental damage, and comes from natural resources like water, sun, and wind.

Green energy can be loosely defined as energy from renewable or sustainable sources; for instance, wind power, solar energy, biomass energy, and hydro power. There are also "waste to energy" projects where a large proportion of the energy comes from biomass (or plant material), although using waste as a fuel for power generation may not be very sustainable.

Equally, while small scale hydro power is considered renewable, the environmental impacts of large scale hydro make it difficult to exploit in an eco-friendly way.

The information provided by suppliers about these different choices is not always transparent and consumers are left confused about their environmental benefits, or even how they add to the renewable energy supplied. At the time of writing there is no scheme in place to verify suppliers' claims about the environmental benefits or "greenness" of their choices.

But just because there is plenty of choice for green electricity doesn't mean they are all good choices. In fact many of the so-called green electricity offerings do not stand up well to close scrutiny. For example, less money than you might expect is being spent directly on generating extra power from renewable sources on top of that already legally required of the energy firms.

As a result, consumers may not be making the positive contribution they had hoped for. Friends of the Earth has come to a similar conclusion, leading it to withdraw its online rating system for green energy suppliers.

So, at the moment, opting for a green option tends to mean one of three things:

"Green" source electricity: Where an energy supplier will guarantee to buy a percentage of electricity from a renewable generator to match every unit of electricity used by the customer.

Here's an idea for you...

Getting bogged down by all the confusing deals and information put out by different utility suppliers? You can save yourself a lot of legwork by getting online and accessing the Department of Energy's Green Power website (www.eere.energy .gov/greenpower). You can then opt for a supplier that prioritizes environmental concerns and offers cleaner energy, so you can be getting greener power within days.

"Green" fund: Tariffs designed to support the building of new renewable sources of electricity generation, environmental causes, or new research and development projects.

Carbon offset: Tariffs help reduce or offset the carbon dioxide emissions or carbon footprint.

Why not think about generating your own power? Find out about alternative methods in IDEA 15, *Earth, wind, and water.*

Try another idea...

There is very little consensus when it comes to green energy. The best way to judge a supply offer is to ask whether it is using any extra cost paid by consumers to invest in new renewable electricity sources. And what kind of sources is it using?

You can also think about installing your own off-grid power in your home, for example by installing a photovoltaic (PV) panel. Or you could buy shares in a locally based renewable energy plan, such as a community wind or hydro project.

You should also remember that even if you are buying green electricity, it is important not to waste power by being as energy efficient as possible—a kilowatt not used is the cleanest kilowatt of all!

OTHER WAYS TO GREEN POWER

An ethical power supplier charges all its customers the same price regardless of how they pay. It uses the income generated by direct debit customers to bring down prices for pre-pay and quarterly consumers.

Pre-pay customers will see much lower prices, while direct debit payers will still get competitive prices, plus the knowledge they are helping to improve social justice.

"All things come from earth, and all things end by becoming earth."

XENOPHANES

Defining idea...

Carbon offsetting

Some energy firms will help you offset the CO_2 produced by your home—and your whole lifestyle. The idea is designed to help reduce the impact of your home's annual carbon emissions, and is calculated using your home's energy usage as well as the number of flights and car trips you make per year.

How did it go?

Q   Isn't this just a way of getting us to pay more for normal grid electricity?

A   *Some consumers are concerned that as the electricity comes through the same wires as the national grid, the whole idea of green electricity is something of a con. This isn't true, so long as your green electricity supplier is committed to investing in new renewable electricity capacity, and is not just relying on sources built many years ago. The whole point is to develop new forms of renewable energy that will last for many years into the future, but there is no getting away from the fact that this is going to need a huge amount of financial investment.*

Q   How much does it cost?

A   *Green power usually costs a little more than standard "brown" power (power generated from burning coal). How much more depends on a number of factors, including your provider, where you live, whether or how much of your electricity is off-peak, and how much green power you purchase.*

9

Low-impact home repair

Our appetite for DIY decorating and home repair seems to be insatiable, but before you reach for the paint can, consider the environmental impact of your creative brushstrokes.

Green home repair can save you money, add value to your home, and is kinder to the planet, too.

Has home improvement ever been so popular? Our magazine racks bulge with decorating glossies, house makeover TV programs seem to be on 24/7, and home repair stores are crammed with so many tempting products that it's downright indecent.

Of course we all want our houses to look fabulous, but perhaps it's time to start taking more care on the home front: Some chemicals and materials that come with the fix-up fetish are major pollutants.

Take MDF, or medium density fiberboard, made from wood fibers glued together. It contains formaldehyde, which is an irritant and probable human carcinogen.

Here's an idea for you...

Trust your nose to sniff out the difference between natural paint and hydrocarbon-based paints. Open a can of the latter and a quick whiff will tell you that it contains strong chemicals. But get close to a can of natural paint and your olfactory senses will home in on ingredients such as natural wood resins, plant oils such as linseed or bergamot, earth pigments, and minerals like chalk or clay. Natural paints don't let off VOCs, are a pleasure to use, and can be composted after use to complete the ecological cycle. And if you ditch the usual petrochemical soup you'll be reducing your household's carbon footprint considerably.

Cutting and drilling MDF generates fibrous dust so, to avoid inhaling the stuff, wear face masks, open doors and windows, or, ideally, do it outdoors. (This may also apply to other wood dusts, so watch out if you are sanding floors.) Ideally you would replace MDF or particleboard with wheat board, produced from agricultural waste wheat straw, and containing a harmless soy flour binder.

It's not just MDF that releases volatile organic compounds (VOCs) into the air: Solvent-based paints, adhesives, flooring, particleboard, and many other building products off-gas in this way, too. That fresh paint or new house smell may shout "improvement" to you, but the calling card of these chemicals that can cause headaches, allergic reactions, nausea, and tiredness. Many hardware stores now sell paints, stains, varnishes, and sealers with minimal or low VOC content so always check the label before you buy, or better still, choose water-based products or less toxic alternatives, such as citrus-based paint strippers and solvents.

Watch out, too, if you are fixing up an old house whose surfaces may have once been painted with a potentially harmful lead-based finish. Removing lead-based paint with a blowtorch or sandpaper is a bad idea—it's better simply to paint over the top. You can buy lead-testing kits from hardware stores, or consider getting a professional tester/remover.

Fit your own insulation to save energy, but make sure it's made from natural or recycled materials. Find out how in IDEA 13, *Warm and cozy.*

Try another idea...

Think about other materials you are using as you fix up your home, and especially avoid those that off-gas such as plastic or PVC, and whose manufacturing process is highly toxic.

Restore damaged fittings wherever you can rather than replacing, and use building products made from recycled materials, or reclaimed building materials sourced from salvage yards or online from websites such as eBay. For instance, you could install an eco-kitchen using recycled glass and cast concrete for stylish backsplashes and countertops, and reclaimed wood and steel for cupboards and flooring.

"I don't paint what I see, I paint what I think."
PABLO PICASSO

Defining idea...

Choose "Low E" (low emission) glass for windows. It has an invisible coating to reflect heat back into the room. If you are replacing radiators, place a heat-reflective shelf above them or back with kitchen foil for a similar effect.

Fit reconstituted doors made of recycled hardboard from lumber mill shavings, which are easy to care for and have good heat insulation.

Only buy as much material as you need for the job, especially paint, which doesn't keep well. Don't throw away your solvent after use, as it contaminates the water supply. Let it stand so the sediment can fall to the bottom, then pour off the clean solvent and reuse it. When cleaning water-based paint from brushes and rollers, scrape as much paint as possible onto sheets of newspaper before washing them to minimize the amount of paint flushed down the drain.

"Creativity is the ability to introduce order into the randomness of nature."

ERIC HOFFER

Q **We'd like to replace our vinyl with eco-friendly wooden flooring. Any suggestions?**

How did it go?

A *Bamboo flooring looks great, is water resistant, is harder than oak or maple, and is very sustainable to grow. But if you're after another hardwood, make sure it's from independently certified, well-managed forests. Or try salvaged or reclaimed wood. Other natural alternatives are linoleum, which is made from wood flour, cork, limestone dust, linseed, and resin on jute backing. Natural cork flooring is also toxin-free, noise absorbent, economic, and insulating, and cork is the only tree whose bark regenerates.*

Q **What should I do with leftover paint?**

A *You can donate it to community groups, charities, and schools either through programs set up by hardware stores or local authorities. (The same applies to off-cuts of timber, odd rolls of wallpaper, flooring, and other materials.) Smaller quantities must never be poured down the drain. Instead, let it dry out before placing it in your trash or at your local civic amenity site.*

Q **How do I know if my local hardware store is environmentally friendly?**

A *Ask to see its policy, and if it doesn't have one, shop elsewhere. Responsible retailers should be working toward sustainable supply chains, e.g., wood and paper products from proven, well-managed forests or made from recycled material. They should be cutting back on the waste and energy produced in running their premises and transport fleet, promoting energy efficient appliances, reducing packaging, and updating chemical-based products.*

10

Always read the label

If it comes in a box, can, bottle, package, or canister, it'll have a label on it. So get informed on what's inside your day-to-day household products.

Are we living with a toxic time bomb? No one really knows, but you can cut back on household chemicals by learning about the worst offenders.

These days we shake our heads over the crazy Elizabethan women who cheerfully sported lead-based makeup, the Romans who were poison-metal mad, and the Victorians who advocated smoking for health reasons.

But are twenty-first-century lifestyles any better? Research from bodies such as Greenpeace has found high levels of chemicals in all kinds of common products including children's clothes and toys, household paints, cleaners, computers, carpets, PVC products, cosmetics, shampoos, detergents, and air fresheners.

Some chemicals have been linked to cancer, liver, and kidney damage and reproductive problems, and children and unborn babies are especially vulnerable. But until

Here's an idea for you...

Often the garage is a dumping ground for hazardous materials such as old paints, thinners, adhesives, car oil, methylated spirits, and car batteries. Get into the habit of cleaning it out regularly, and go through each can or bottle to check exactly what it contains. Ask your local authority for advice on disposing of chemical-based products. Ideally the garage should be completely closed off from the rest of the house, but if connected by a door, always keep it shut and the garage well ventilated to release toxic vehicle emissions and chemical off-gassing.

every single potentially nasty chemical is analyzed, we are all playing the guinea pig in a global chemistry experiment.

It's up to you how far you go in avoiding substances—it's almost impossible to be 100 percent green. But the main thing is to be aware, so at least you have the choice. Get into the habit of reading product labels and swapping those that contain toxic stuff for greener alternatives.

COSMETICS AND TOILETRIES

Cosmetics and toiletries can contain a variety of hazardous substances, especially in nail polish, perfumes, hair sprays, household cleaners, and deodorizers.

Avoid:

- Cosmetics, toiletries, and perfumes with synthetic fragrances, usually labeled "parfum" or "fragrance" on the ingredients list.
- Toothpaste, toothbrushes, and mouthwashes containing Triclosan.
- Long-term use of permanent hair dyes, especially those warning of allergic reactions.

HOUSEHOLD GOODS

Be wary of the these products:

- Teflon and other nonstick pans give off toxic fumes if overheated, so use cast iron or stainless steel pans.
- Canned foods have a lining that contains Bisphenol-A, suspected to interact with our hormone systems.
- Products containing Triclosan: certain plastic chopping boards, washcloths, sponges, liquids, soaps, and disinfectants.
- Chemical air fresheners, antibacterials, or heavily scented cleaning products are also on the hit list.

PLASTICS

Try to avoid anything made from soft PVC, which is hard to recycle and may contain phthalates, widespread contaminants in the global environment and known to disrupt the endocrine system. Look out for packaging stamped with "PVC 3," or in the recycling triangle with the number 3.

Polycarbonate plastic (PC) contains bisphenol A, which is a hormone-disrupting chemical. Polycarbonate plastics can often be identified by looking on the packaging for "PC7" or looking inside the recycling triangle for the number 7.

For more on how to detox your home, take a look at IDEA 22, _Let's step outside_.

Try another idea...

"Feelings are like chemicals, the more you analyze them the worse they smell."

CHARLES KINGSLEY

Defining idea...

47

DECORATING MATERIALS

Many household paints give off dangerous fumes as they dry. Most paints are now labeled to tell you how many VOCs (fumes) they give off—look for those marked "low" or "minimal" VOC content. Use water-based paints where possible.

WORST CULPRITS

- Artificial musks are used in many toiletries and cleaning products, usually described as "parfum" or "fragrance" on labels. They are bioaccumulative contaminants in the environment.
- Bisphenol A is a hormone disrupting chemical found in some polycarbonate plastic, used for baby feeding bottles, refillable water bottles, food containers, CDs and DVDs, and electrical appliances.
- Brominated flame retardants (BFRs) are found in plastics, textiles, furniture, and electrical appliances, and are suspected hormone disrupters.
- Parabens are preservatives found in most cosmetics. They have also been found to mimic estrogen, and have been found in breast cancer tumors. They are known skin and eye irritants, and have also been linked to sperm damage in males.
- Phthalates are added to PVC plastics to make them pliable, and to a wide range of cosmetics. They are associated with liver, kidney, and testicular damage.
- Triclosan is a strong antibacterial used in toothpastes, mouthwashes, soaps, deodorants, dishcloths, and chopping boards. There are claims that its widespread use is leading to risks to the environment and human health.

Q   **Surely the government wouldn't allow harmful chemicals in toiletries and other common products, would it?**

How did it go?

A   *It's a question of degree—legislation is designed to cut back on the worst of toxic chemicals but there are still plenty in use whose effects on our bodies are yet to be clarified. Here's one small example: Around 90 percent of all commercial shampoos and personal care products (including tooth-pastes) use a cheap foaming agent called sodium laurel sulphate, aka sodium lauryl sulphate or sodium laureth sulphate, which are all known irritants and possibly even carcinogens. I like to play it safe and buy SLS-free shampoo and toothpaste.*

Q   **How do I know how much of a substance is contained in a product?**

A   *Ingredients are always listed in order, so the nearer to the top of the list a substance is, the greater its quantity.*

Q   **Where can I find out more about hidden chemicals in the home?**

A   *A good starting place is one of the large environmental organizations such as Greenpeace (www.greenpeace.org), who have carried out extensive research into this sort of thing. Worldwide Fund for Nature (www.panda .org) and Friends of the Earth (www.foe.org) also have lots of information about chemicals and other toxins in the home.*

11

The low-impact consumer

A new kind of consumer has been born, and the pared-down approach means spending less and getting things for free.

Ever get the feeling that you're on a consumer treadmill? Jump off now and hit the ground running.

The eco-movement has spawned a whole new vocabulary, and one of the new buzzwords is "freegan" (free + vegan). Dining on food leftovers from Dumpsters may have once been the preserve of tramps, but for some it is now more of a lifestyle choice. Greener-than-thou freegans veer away from consumerism and instead scavenge around to meet their needs, including finding food thrown out by shops and restaurants.

And why not? Supermarkets dump 5 percent of their food, most of it completely fit for consumption, as a faster, cheaper option than giving it away. The freegan movement is especially popular in New York, where people regularly go through the trash bins together on "trash tours," but it is becoming more widespread elsewhere.

If you want to try your hand as a freegan, stick to a few basic rules:

Here's an idea for you...

Feeling bold—and hungry? Then try being a freegan for a week, and discover firsthand how much commercial food waste goes on. (A freegan could be described as a scavenger with a conscience, someone who survives on other people's leftovers.) Once you get going on your foraging mission you'll be astonished at how much food is dumped behind shops, markets, and restaurants at the end of each day, much of it fit for consumption but all destined for the local landfill site. If you're squeamish you don't have to eat what you salvage—although you certainly could—but it'll give you a snapshot of how much food is routinely thrown out by our health and safety-obsessed society.

- Wear gloves when you scavenge, and use a flashlight at night.
- Don't ignore signs that say "No Trespassing."
- Leave the trash can in the same condition as you found it.
- Examine use-by dates, and stick to packaged or bagged goods if you're not sure about something.
- Wash all the items you find before eating.
- Small to medium shops usually provide richer pickings than large supermarkets, which tend to lock up Dumpsters.

PRECYCLING

You can cut down on waste by "precycling," preventing waste before it happens: bringing your own packaging, buying in bulk, avoiding junk mail and disposables, extending the life of what you've got, and not buying what you don't need.

Ardent precyclers carry their own little kit: a washable container, a set of cutlery, a cloth napkin or handkerchief, a bottle of water, and a reusable shopping bag.

FREECYCLING

If you don't want it, pass it on. There are several free goods swapping web-based organizations, notably Freecycle (www.freecycle.org), made up of many local groups across the world. Freecycle groups match people who have things they want to get rid of with people who can use them, keeping usable items out of landfills, reducing consumerism, and lessening the impact on the earth.

Recycling should be part of your day-to-day routine. Get the lowdown in IDEA 4, *Once more with feeling.*

Try another idea…

DUMPSTERS

Dumpsters outside houses or other buildings undergoing renovation may just seem full of junk, but to the dedicated low-impact consumer they are a treasure chest for "Dumpster diving." You can usually assume that anything in a Dumpster isn't wanted, but if you're not sure ask the property owner before carting it away.

WILD FORAGING

Instead of buying industrially grown, pesticide sprayed foods shipped halfway around the world, get back to your roots and find and harvest food growing wild in your own community.

FREE EVENTS

Make the most of free-for-all events where you can exchange goods instead of discard-

"I used to sell furniture for a living. The trouble was, it was my own."

LES DAWSON

Defining idea…

ing them, share skills, give presents, eat food, dance, listen to music, sing, and generally have fun.

CARPOOLING

Whether it's called ride-sharing or carpooling, it pretty much comes down to the same thing—sharing a car for a journey rather than driving alone. The environmental benefits are obvious, as are the financial ones. The Internet is a good place to start to find out about local programs, or your city council may have information.

ALLOTMENTS AND COMMUNITY GARDENS

Once you've paid the rent for your patch, everything you grow in your allotment is your own, meaning you can have a year-round supply of fresh fruit and vegetables completely free.

BICYCLE COLLECTIVES

Find out about groups that facilitate community sharing of bicycles, restore found and broken bikes, and teach people how to do their own bike repairs.

Q   How can I survive without my creature comforts?

How did it go?

A   *If the thought scares you, why not give it a try for a day? Take inspiration from Buy Nothing Day, an international event where you challenge your-self, your family, and your friends to switch off from shopping for twenty-four hours. In Canada and the United States it's the Friday after Thanksgiving, while in Europe it falls on the last Saturday in November. The challenge is to try simple living for a day, spending time with family and friends rather than spending money on them. It's surprisingly challenging to last twenty-four hours without spending any money, but if you manage it you'll have a mini shopping detox and appreciate how much it uses up your free time.*

Q   Isn't there a limit to what you can get for nothing?

A   *Well, some hard-core freegans would beg to differ! But if life as a scav-enger doesn't appeal, take it down a level. You can still partially opt out of consumerism by buying secondhand, which helps to extend the life of perfectly acceptable goods. There is no shortage of excellent junk shops, yard sales, auction websites such as eBay, flea markets, and bring-and-buy sales. And if you buy from charity, another bonus is that your money ends up going to a deserving cause. Once you see the bargains to be had there's no turning back!*

12

Petal power

Get in touch with your inner horticulturalist and go green, literally, by splurging on detoxifying houseplants for your home.

Houseplants add greenery and character to a room, provide a mini carbon offsetting program, and improve your health and well-being.

Don't you just love it when something truly pleasurable, natural, and harmless is given the green light by the experts?

The psychological and health benefits of houseplants have been unofficially recognized since ancient times, but when an organization such as NASA starts churning out reports that give this scientific weight, you know that some big issues are at stake. From its research into air pollution inside sealed space habitats, NASA discovered that ordinary houseplants have amazing air purification capabilities.

And what works inside a spacecraft also works in your home. Nature created the human/plant world in balance, so that each supplies the other's needs—we give plants carbon dioxide when we breathe out, and they give us oxygen. Plants decrease carbon dioxide concentrations and air temperatures in buildings as well as raising humidity. If we all filled our homes with houseplants, it would go a little way toward offsetting some of the carbon dioxide each house inevitably produces, which in turn contributes to global warming.

Modern synthetic furnishings, computers, and electrical equipment, together with everyday substances such as cleaning materials, emit various harmful gases in small quantities. People who are sensitive can suffer from dizziness, nausea, breathing problems, and more.

Here's an idea for you…

Look after your houseplants and maximize their detox properties. Place them in a brightly lit position out of direct sunlight and drafts, and feed them regularly to give them the energy to flower, produce new roots, and encourage healthy leaf growth. Most houseplants enjoy a regular misting of lukewarm water to prevent drying leaf tips, to clean the leaves, and to keep the plants breathing well. Plants with broad glossy leaves appreciate an occasional wipe over with a damp cloth; their "lungs" are in the leaf surface and a layer of dust will stop them from breathing. Whether or not you want to have the occasional chat, too, is entirely up to you!

NASA found that foliage plants had an excellent ability to remove VOCs and stop people from experiencing those queasy or "sick building" feelings without being harmed themselves. Spider plants, for example, can remove up to 96 percent of carbon monoxide, a toxic exhaust gas. Other health-giving plants that are also easy to look after include chrysanthemums, ivy, and dracaena.

As a bonus, studies have shown that living plants have a beneficial psychological effect; for instance, patients in hospitals recover faster when plants are present.

These are some of the most effective detoxifiers.

- Dragon tree (dracaena)
- Ivy
- Ficus, either weeping fig or the sturdy rubber plant

- Philodendron
- Spider plant
- Peace lily
- Ferns, all varieties
- Chrysanthemums
- Gerbera
- Palms

Houseplants may pave the way for a greener living space, so read IDEA 5, *Detox your home*, **for more ideas.**

Try another idea...

Use the same kind care as you would for outdoor gardening: Choose the right plants for your conditions, plant them in healthy soil, give them fertilizer and water properly, and keep an eye on things.

Don't overwater your plants; only give them a drink when the top layer of soil is dry. Plants growing in clay containers dry out faster than those in plastic pots. Also, plants growing in direct light need water more frequently than those in darker places, and they will need more water during the summer when they are actively growing.

Don't kill your plants with food, either, as overfeeding makes them weak and susceptible to disease. Only feed them during the active growing season.

Avoid the synthetic kinds of fertilizers, and instead use a weak but balanced dilution of fish and seaweed fertilizer, ideally organic. Frequent weak applications of fertilizer are better than infrequent heavy applications for houseplants.

"Little flower—but if I could understand
What you are, root and all, and all in all,
I should know what God and man is."

TENNYSON

Defining idea...

Repot your plants about once every other year. Do it in the spring or summer when the plants are actively growing.

Q **Will my dingy little apartment really support life—other than my own, of course?**

A *Pick the right houseplant, and the answer's yes. Rule number one is making sure they suit the conditions of your home. A sun-loving cactus will struggle in a dark room, whereas a variety originally from a dense tropical canopy such as* Epipremnium aureum *(devil's ivy) or* Monstera delicosa *(Swiss cheese plant) may thrive. Other hard-to-kill detoxing plants that won't mind a little gloom include dragon tree, ivy, peace lily, and aspidistra.*

Q **How can I buy houseplants from sustainable sources?**

A *It isn't always easy to tell how or where a houseplant has been grown, but a new initiative should change this. The Fair Flowers Fair Plants (FFP) organization (www.fairflowersfairplants.com) is the new international body whose remit is to monitor and check ethical standards, so look out for the FFP label when buying flowers and plants. Labeled plants should be guaranteed to originate from growers who fulfill high standards of ethical growing.*

Q **Where should my houseplants be placed for the most benefit?**

A *If you want to benefit fully from their detox properties, plants should live within your personal breathing zone, so put them next to the television seating area, computer, or bed. Otherwise, rooms with either morning or afternoon sun are usually the best place for thriving houseplants. Most won't tolerate long periods of direct sunlight and don't like strong heat (radiators, fan heaters, and so on) or chilly drafts. When it comes to quantity, the more the merrier—try to host at least two to three plants per 100 square feet.*

13

Warm and cozy

Feel like a penny-pincher if you go around turning off the lights? Well, don't! It's a sign you're saving energy and shrinking your carbon footprint.

We all know that saving gas and electricity and conserving heat helps reduce global warming. But how many of us do it on a day-to-day basis?

Now be honest—is your home really as energy-wise as it ought to be? You don't have to be a genius to figure out that if you cut back on fuel usage you will save yourself money, and obviously it has environmental benefits, too.

There are basically two biggies when it comes to saving energy: One, use less power, and two, keep the heat in.

We've all heard the one about turning your thermostat down by 1 degree and installing energy-saving bulbs, but there are lots of other small measures you can take that add up to a big saving in fuel—and money.

Insulation is the key to any ecologically sound home. Heat loss through walls and roofs can account for as much as 80 percent of heating costs. Insulating cavity walls

Here's an idea for you...

Don't feel you have to insulate your entire home in one shot, as it can be a costly job. Make a start by heat-proofing your favorite rooms; for example, the kitchen or the living room. And if double glazing or cavity wall insulation is out of your reach, start off with cheap measures such as thick curtains or window sealants. To gauge how drafty a room is, simply hold up the palm of your hand to the window, floorboards, or closed door and feel the change in temperature; if cold air is coming in, warm air is going out! Or hold up a piece of ribbon and watch it flutter.

and attics makes the most difference. Hot water tanks can be fitted with an inexpensive insulating jacket. You can also wrap hot water pipes to stop heat from escaping.

Your home could be losing up to 20 percent of its heat through single glazed and poorly insulated window frames. Double glazing can cut these losses by over a half. But if you decide to replace, try to use Forest Stewardship–approved wood, not PVC, which is high in toxins and hard to recycle.

It costs next to nothing to eliminate drafts and wasted heat. Fix a brush or seal on your exterior doors, fill gaps in floorboards and skirting, and have thick curtains to insulate windows. But don't suffocate! Open fireplaces, gas heaters, or boilers with flues need some ventilation to stop toxic buildup.

Watch how much hot water you waste. Always turn off hot water taps when you're not using them; a dripping hot water tap wastes enough hot water over a week to fill half a bath. An ordinary shower uses less than half of the water needed for a bath. Look at the water temperature, too; it doesn't need to be set higher than 140 degrees F.

Match the right size pan to the amount of food you're cooking and keep lids on. Only use as much water as you need, including inside kettles.

APPLIANCES

Fridges are on 24/7 so they use a huge amount of power. Always close the door quickly to stop cold air from escaping and don't put hot or warm food straight into the fridge. Leave a good gap between fridges and ovens or boilers.

A new breed of gadgets can help you cut your energy costs. Find out how in IDEA 20, *Green gadgets*.

Try another idea…

With washing machines, tumble dryers, and dishwashers, always wash a full load or use a half-load or economy program at the lowest temperature you can get away with.

Save energy by turning off your dishwasher before it completes its drying cycle, leaving the heat inside to do the work.

Replace old appliances with energy-saving models displaying an appropriate logo or certification.

If your furnace is over fifteen years old, consider replacing it with a high-efficiency condensing type. They can help you save up to a third on your heating bills and even more if you upgrade to modern controls.

Don't leave appliances, such as TVs, stereos, and DVD players on standby, or cell phones or laptops on charge unnecessarily.

"We are living on this planet as if we had another one to go to."

TERRI SWEARINGEN,
environmental campaigner

Defining idea…

Q   I'm going to tackle my attic and get it fully insulated—at last! What's the best material to use?

A   *It can take more energy to manufacture insulation than you will ever save. There are green alternatives, though, such as insulation made from recycled newspapers or wool. Wool is especially good, reducing condensation and absorbing sound and toxins. Other products such as Termex and Warmcel are made from fire-retarded waste newspaper and use around 90 percent less energy in their manufacture than conventional materials.*

Q   How can I figure out how much energy I am saving?

A   *Get to know your kilowattage by checking your bills and meter. For both electricity and gas you will be charged per kilowatt hour of energy you use, whose tally is shown on the meters in your home and calculated over a certain period. There are also portable plug-in devices that can do the hard work for you.*

Q   Is it more economical to leave my heating on twenty-four hours a day in the winter?

A   *Furnaces do use more power initially to heat from cold, but the cost of this initial burst of energy is far outweighed by the cost of keeping it running all the time. Instead, program your heating system so that it comes on when you need it most, usually first thing in the morning and in the evening.*

14

Burn naturally

Ah, nothing beats the warmth of an open fire. But hold on—your yen for a den fragrant with wood smoke might be doing nasty things to the air around you.

It's a rare case of "green" not being clean— you need to burn old, well-seasoned wood to avoid hurtling harmful particles into your neighborhood.

What could be nicer than snuggling down with a good book beside an open fire? More and more of us are unblocking old fireplaces or flues and getting down and dirty in the wood pile. Wood is a fantastically versatile fuel and can be burned in many different forms and in loads of different appliances. It can heat one room or the whole house; it can produce hot water and heat for cooking.

But hold your hearthside horses—if you want an open fire you're living with massive heat loss. As much as 90 percent of the heat will go straight up the chimney! Open fires also increase drafts, drawing seventeen cubic meters of air per minute up the flue. In terms of efficiency, a closed wood burner is far better, especially the new breed of clean-burning stoves.

Bear in mind that burning anything will release some emissions: carbon dioxide and traces of carbon monoxide, particulates, and volatile organic compounds.

Logs are better than coal in this respect, though, as they are from a renewable source in the sense that you are only releasing the carbon dioxide that was absorbed as the tree grew.

Here's an idea for you...

Learn about different kinds of wood before you burn them. The heavier and denser the wood, the longer it will burn. Hardwoods such as oak or beech tend to be denser than softwoods (e.g., pine and spruce). But it can be tricky to burn these very dense hardwoods, so it is usually best to combine them with another type of wood. Softwoods tend to catch easily and burn quickly, so are good for kindling but don't have much staying power otherwise. Some species like spruce and horse chestnut spit badly, making them unpleasant in an open fire. Good woods to burn are ash, beech, hornbeam, hawthorn, crab apple, and wild cherry.

Wood needs plenty of air to burn cleanly, and this means a sound, clear chimney that should be swept annually to avoid the risk of it catching fire and of carbon monoxide poisoning, which can happen with blockages or a lack of ventilation.

These are some of the golden rules for a warm, environmentally sound fire:

- Burn small, hot fires using seasoned wood, ideally with logs around 4–6 inches in diameter.
- Source logs locally, e.g., from a local tree surgeon, or from dead trees that have fallen.
- Never burn trash, plastics, glossy paper or polystyrene, treated or painted wood, particleboard, or plywood.

- Store wood outside, off the ground, and covered. Bringing green wood indoors to dry can cause the growth of mold spores indoors, which could trigger allergies.
- Make sure the fire is getting enough air—check that the air inlet is open wide enough to keep the fire burning briskly and with minimum smoke.
- Put old ash to good use in your compost heap. It's high in potash and a good garden fertilizer.
- Install a carbon monoxide detector and a smoke alarm in any room where wood or any other fuel is burned.

Burning wood is a low carbon form of heating, but there are others you can find out about in IDEA 15, *Earth, wind, and water.*

Try another idea...

PELLET STOVES

Pellet stoves are the new black in wood-burning terms. They look similar to traditional wood burning stoves but use thermostatic controls and fans to distribute warm air around the room. They have many of the advantages of fossil fuel heating systems, such as efficiency and heat distribution but minus the environmental damage. They can hold enough fuel for a few days and have an ash pan that needs to be emptied no more than once a month to once a year so they are highly practical. The pellets, a form of bioenergy, are usually made from timber waste from sawmills, which is processed to be carbon neutral and so is less harmful to the environment than other fossil fuels. Pellet stoves must be installed by a specialist.

"It is folly to punish your neighbor by fire when you live next door."

ESKIMO PROVERB

Defining idea...

67

How did it go?

Q   **Why does wood need to be seasoned?**

A   *The key to burning better is burning older—you should only burn wood that has been cut for at least a year and allowed to dry out. Freshly cut or "green" wood can be up to 80 percent water, while well seasoned firewood generally has a moisture content of 20 percent or less, making it burn faster, hotter, and cleaner. If your wood is cut a year to eighteen months in advance and properly stacked, the sun and wind will get rid of the moisture for you. Green wood will smolder rather than burn, so less heat will be delivered into your home, more creosote will be deposited in your chimney, and more smoke into the atmosphere and your lungs.*

Q   **I love the idea of an open fire but wonder whether a stove might be more practical. I live in the city, so which is best?**

A   *An open fire looks and feels great, but isn't that efficient and in some built-up areas you are required to burn smokeless fuel. A better bet is a certified clean-burning wood stove, which is likely to be around 70 percent efficient and can use wood in a smokeless zone. Some stoves can also be fitted with back boilers to heat one or more radiators or domestic hot water. If your budget stretches to a new stove, pellet stoves and boilers produce very low emissions yet are highly efficient.*

15

Earth, wind, and water

Don't just plug in, turn on, and zone out—why not go "off grid" and investigate some alternative energy supplies?

Want to see your household fuel bills plummet? Then harness natural energy sources such as earth, wind, water, and sun, and go green at the same time.

What could be better than knowing that the energy you use in your home is simply the by-product of the earth's own natural forces? Renewable energy, such as solar and wind power, can be used without depleting natural resources and with minimal pollution.

And better still, if you produce excess energy you can sell it back to the national grid, saving you even more money.

There are several different kinds of microgeneration (energy created on a bite-size basis), some better for domestic use than others. But, whatever gives you a buzz, it's usually best to get it installed by professionals—and do be realistic about its energy output. In some cases you'll be looking at twenty years–plus to recoup your costs. Also, check out any building restrictions and rules with your local authority, and while you're at it, ask them (or your power suppliers) about any grants available.

HERE COMES THE SUN

There are basically two kinds of solar power: solar water heating system, which simply heats a tank of water; and solar photovoltaic (PV), which uses sunlight to create electricity to run appliances and lighting.

The easiest for most householders is a solar water heating system, which is very low maintenance and can provide about half of your domestic hot water needs over the year. You'll need a backup system in the winter, though, probably from your existing central heating boiler.

Here's an idea for you...

One cost-effective way of finding your way through the alternative energy maze is to bring in a professional eco-consultant or environmental auditor who can give you the lowdown on your individual potential in energy saving. You may have to pay them a fee, but you're sure to get that back and more when your utility bills plummet! An auditor can talk you through the pros and cons of heavy-duty hardware such as wind turbines and ground source pumps, where it's all too easy to get bogged down in an information overload.

Roof-mounted solar panels collect heat from the sun's radiation; this heat is transferred into a hot water system, which is stored in a tank. The system you end up with depends on factors such as the area of south-facing roof, the existing water heating system, and, of course, your budget.

Solar photovoltaic (PV) requires only daylight—not direct sunlight—to generate electricity, and uses cells made of a semi-conducting material, usually silicon, to convert solar radiation into electricity. PV systems generate no greenhouse gases and can be used on any building with a strong enough roof or wall that faces within 90 degrees of south, as long as no other buildings or large trees overshadow it.

Prices for PV systems vary, depending on the size of the system to be installed, the type of PV cell used, and the nature of the building that houses the PV. The more juice you want, the bigger the system.

MICRO WIND TURBINES

There has been a lot of hype around micro wind turbines, although the idea is straightforward enough: They use the wind's forces to spin aerodynamic blades that turn a rotor to create electricity. But to generate plentiful power and recoup your costs they need to sit in a consistently windy spot, preferably in a remote rural area with no buildings or trees nearby that might interfere with the wind force.

To determine your home's potential you would ideally assess the speed and direction of the wind over a period, perhaps up to a year. Not something to be undertaken lightly! Planning issues such as visual impact, noise, and conservation rules also have to be considered.

SMALL-SCALE HYDRO

Using the flow of water around a turbine (waterwheel) to generate energy is probably the oldest form of renewable energy. Hydropower produces no waste products during operation and, once up and running, it's free.

Suitable sites include mountainous spots where there are fast-flowing streams, and lowland areas with wide rivers. Small hydro systems can supply electricity directly to homes or can be used to charge batteries or as a backup to a diesel generator.

Is your energy supplier as green as you'd like it to be? Find out how to switch utilities in IDEA 8, *You've got the power.*

Try another idea...

"Adapt or perish, now as ever, is Nature's inexorable imperative."

H. G. WELLS

Defining idea...

71

GROUND SOURCE HEAT PUMPS

Ground source heat pumps (GSHPs) make use of energy stored in the earth through a series of pumps and pipes. The only energy used by GSHP systems is electricity for the pumps, but this should easily be outweighed by the thermal energy or heat generated.

GSHP systems can be pricey to install but they have very low maintenance costs and should last at least twenty years. They work best with heating systems designed to run at a lower water temperature; for example, underfloor heating.

How did
it go?

Q   I love the idea of renewable energy but isn't it all a little pricey?

A   You may have to fork out in initial costs but you will get it all back and more as your fuel bills go down. Technology is improving all the time, and in most cases your new systems should pay for themselves eventually. And you may be able to get a grant to help toward the cost.

Q   Will installing renewable energy measures affect the value of my home?

A   Yes—it should go up! The more people become aware of green issues, the more they're buying into environmental home improvements. There is also increasingly a certain amount of kudos attached to eco-homes, and, in some cases, tax benefits. And even if you don't recoup your entire cost, going green should certainly make your home more saleable. After all, everyone likes the idea of cut-price fuel bills!

16

Good wood

Wonderful natural wood is an asset to any home as long as it comes from sustainable sources.

"Buy with care, treat it fair" should be your mantra when it comes to all things wooden.

Glossy, synthetic materials may proliferate in the twenty-first-century home, but there's nothing like real, natural wood for beauty, durability, and versatility. Wood is warm in winter and helps keep rooms cool in the summer, it lends itself to both modern and contemporary styles, and conditioned with natural nontoxic waxes or oils, such as linseed, it will last you a lifetime.

While we're not yet at the stage of treating wood as a rare commodity, we do need to go easy on this most precious of resources.

With ancient forests worldwide being chopped down faster than you can say "matchstick," it's up to you to make sure that it comes from a properly managed forest. Forests contain as much as 90 percent of the world's terrestrial biodiversity. Forests purify the air we breathe, provide lifesaving medicines, and are key to controlling soil erosion and preventing flooding. But approximately half of the Earth's original forest cover has been cut down and, of the half that remains, only around one tenth is protected, and most of this is badly managed.

Here's an idea for you...

Some of the best quality wooden flooring (and other fittings) is vintage stuff that is found in reclamation or salvage yards. Get to know your local suppliers or scour trading websites like eBay for good secondhand buys. Older wood still in good condition will have stood the test of time; Victorian pine floors, for instance, were originally made from very dense first growth forest timber, far superior to most new wood sold these days. Another alternative is to buy recycled wood products. That way you know you're not using up natural resources, but instead just using existing materials.

You can do your part by increasing demand for certified timber, particularly for tropical hardwoods that are used widely in garden furniture. If you're buying new wood, source products that are Forest Stewardship Council (FSC) certified.

The FSC is an international organization that promotes care of the world's forests. FSC certification guarantees your timber comes from a well-managed forest. Although there are many certification initiatives around, the FSC is the only program that fulfills all requirements for a credible plan, and is the only one recommended by Fauna & Flora International and Friends of the Earth.

It's not just the tropics that suffer. The supposedly lower-risk forests of Scandinavia and Canada have also felt the effects of logging and the drainage of peat bogs and felling of ancient forest to clear the way for new, managed plantations. Without certification of timber products sourced from these areas, consumers cannot be reassured by a sustainability logo. And without the logo, customers cannot express a collective consumer pull.

Defining idea...

"Forests are the lungs of our land."

FRANKLIN D. ROOSEVELT

Think about how the timber reached the shop, too. Timber from closer to home requires less transportation and the carbon dioxide (CO_2) produced by traffic has a dramatic effect on climate change. The farther the travel, the higher the CO_2 emissions!

Wood is a highly recyclable material but so are many others—see what else can be used again and again in IDEA 4, *Once more with feeling.*

Try another idea…

REPAIR, RESTORE, OR ADAPT

Timber makes up as much as 10 percent of material dumped in public waste sites but most of it could be used again. Obviously it's even more environmentally sound to simply repair, restore, or adapt a wooden product you already have. You may need to get a pro in for the job, but it could still be cheaper than buying something new and it's far better for the world's forests.

It's worth thinking whether friends or neighbors could use the spare timber from your house or garden, or perhaps a local school or community group would appreciate timber off-cuts from your home improvement projects.

Some quality timber items, such as doors, fireplaces, and kitchen units might be worth selling through an ad in a local shop or newspaper, or via online shopping portals, such as eBay.

"What we are doing to the forests of the world is but a mirror reflection of what we are doing to ourselves and to one another."

MAHATMA GANDHI

Defining idea…

How did it go?

Q   Should I avoid buying tropical hardwood?

A   *Buying tropical woods doesn't necessarily equate with environmental damage if the product has a sustainable stamp—it could, after all, be the product of a properly managed and funded project that helps local communities develop responsible woodland practices. Any product tied in to a reputable project should carry some kind of certification, the best being from the Forest Stewardship Council. Forest certification is growing but it's costly to implement at the moment—only 10 percent of global timber production is independently certified, much of this originating from Europe and North America. It can take years to work toward certification, so in the meantime the least you can do is find out whether the supplier of the wood is practicing good forest management and working toward certification.*

Q   Wood is green, we're told, yet so is double glazing. So where on earth does that leave us with choosing window frames?

A   *According to the WWF, you're better off choosing wooden windows as they are better for the environment than PVC. WWF found that PVC windows were less sustainable and more hazardous than wood. Around half of PVC is made from a nonrenewable source, oil. PVC windows also generate more waste and use eight times more energy to manufacture than timber windows, it says. If you can afford them, go for double-glazed wooden windows as they combine good insulation properties and use a sustainable material.*

17

If in drought...

Ever stopped to think about how much water you're wasting? Even if you don't live in a drought-ridden area, it's still prudent to cut back on the amount of H$_2$O that goes down the drain.

Some parts of the planet are becoming near deserts, so we must act now to conserve one of life's most essential and precious elements: water.

Water is something that many of us take for granted, not thinking twice before lazing back in a hot bath at the end of a hard day or carelessly leaving the sprinkler on in the garden.

But recent hot summers have left water restrictions in place worldwide, and few have failed to get the message that water is fast becoming a luxury rather than something we take for granted.

Global water consumption has risen almost tenfold in the last century, and UNESCO has predicted that by 2020 water shortage will be a major worldwide problem, bringing with it disease, malnourishment, crop failure, and environmental damage. So each and every one of us needs to take responsibility for the amount of water we consume.

SAVING WATER IN THE KITCHEN AND LAUNDRY

■ One of the easiest ways of saving water in the kitchen/laundry is to install a water-efficient dishwasher and washing machine and ensure that you fill them right up each time.

Here's an idea for you...

Think before you flush. Toilets use about 30 percent of the total water used in a household, and the older your tank, the more water you waste, with the worst offenders flushing away a whopping thirteen liters of water each time you pull the handle! (Modern dual-flush toilets use six liters for a full flush and four liters with a "mini" flush.) If your toilet is more than a few years old, install a tank displacement device, which is basically an inflated plastic bag that sits inside the tank and displaces about one liter of water every time you flush. It doesn't sound like much, but when you think that the average household flushes up to 5,000 times per year, that's an awful lot of water!

■ If you wash by hand, use minimum detergent to cut back on rinsing, and use a plugged sink or a bowl of water.

■ Use only as much water as you need in kettles or saucepans to cut your electricity costs at the same time.

■ Flow-controlled aerators for taps are simple devices that you fit into existing tap nozzles, and mix air with water under pressure as it emerges from the tap without affecting the flow rate. They can be bought at most hardware and housewares stores, are inexpensive, and can halve water flow.

■ Try to capture "warm-up" water for use on plants, rinsing dishes, washing fruits and vegetables, or other cleaning jobs.

■ Insulate hot water pipes so that you need to run less water before it heats up. Equally, keep a bottle of drinking water in the refrigerator so you don't need to run the tap until the water is cold enough.

■ Don't use a garbage-disposal unit. They use about thirty liters of water per day and send a lot of extra junk into the sewers. Compost what you can and trash the rest.

BATHROOM

- Take showers rather than baths, and keep them short; use a timer if you have a large family. Power showers can use more water than a bath in less than five minutes, though!
- Turn the tap off when brushing your teeth or shaving. A running tap uses about five liters of water per minute.
- Install a water efficient showerhead and toilet tank.

OUTSIDE

- Install a rainwater tank that collects runoff from roofs and gutters for garden use, or ask your local government about getting it connected to the toilet for flushing.
- If you're watering the garden, make sure you only water plants and lawns, not paths, paving, and buildings.
- Use a broom or rake to clean outdoor paths and paving instead of hosing them down with water.
- If you have a pool, install a cover to reduce evaporation, and persuade pool users to cut back on overexuberant splashing.
- Wash your car sparingly, reusing water from inside, or, if you don't have to drive too far, visit a commercial car wash that recycles wash water.

Gardens should be green but we still need to use water sparingly. Read **IDEA 32, *The low-water garden*, for tips on how.**

Try another idea...

"The frog does not drink up the pond in which it lives."
CHINESE PROVERB

Defining idea...

How did
it go?

**Q   I hate to think of the waste when I see water disappearing down
the drain after a bath or shower. Could I reuse it?**

A   *Waste water from baths and showers is called graywater, and contains
bacteria that may include disease-causing organisms that multiply rapidly.
It would usually be OK for the garden if used immediately, or for cleaning cars, but not much else unless decontaminated. You can get a special
recycling system installed by a plumber (check with local authorities first
though). Graywater can also be hard to collect, so you may be better off
using water left over from washing vegetables or rinsing things, or collecting water that runs off while it warms up, such as when taking a shower.*

Q   How can I become more water aware?

A   *The best way to save water is to make friends with your water meter, if
you have one, to help you keep tabs on just how much water you and your
family use. Get into the habit of reading your meter, and use it to check for
leaks, drips, and broken pipes—dripping taps can waste 30–200 liters of
water per day! Monitor the dials on the water meter when you're sure no
water is being used inside or out, perhaps just before you go to bed and
again when you get up. Any change shows you probably have a leak, so
locate the problem quickly and repair it.*

18

Shop smart

Ethical shopping—what is it and how can you do it? The answers are trickling in slower than organic honey.

Local or fair-trade; organic or free-range; line-caught or netted? No wonder a trip to the grocery store gives your conscience a battering.

Eco-shopping means knowing more than just what's on your grocery list.

On the one hand, we're told that we should eat food that is locally produced and not flown hundreds of miles; on the other we're under pressure to support producers in faraway developing countries. We're expected to know the difference between organic and free-range foods, stay abreast of flashpoints (palm oil, bluefin tuna, PVC), and only buy goods with certain eco-labels attached.

Confusing? Of course.

Guilt making? You bet.

To me, as the rights and wrongs of living green seem to be shifting faster than the sands in the Sahara, the best starting point is simply to be informed about what you buy.

Here's an idea for you... **Try this as an exercise: Spend one week shopping only at your neighborhood stores and markets, and see how different it makes you feel. Instead of the rushed, anonymous experience of racing around the supermarket aisles, enjoy the shopkeeper's personal attention, tried and trusted goods, and pride in their stock. Ask to look, feel, taste, and smell, too—and leave the car behind if you can or share with a friend. Supermarkets may be cheaper to shop at than local retailers, as they can use their mighty buying power, but give the little guys a chance, too!**

Get to know what's inside the product you're buying; whether it's organic or not; how it is produced and where; and how it is delivered.

To some extent you have to pick your battles. If your main concern is climate change, then you'll want to know how far your goods have traveled. (Some retailers are now providing point-of-sale freighting information.) If you're worried about chemicals, then you'll go for organic and natural. If you hate the thought of producers getting a raw deal you'll buy fair-trade. And if you deplore the way that supermarket giants have squeezed supply chains and taken over neighborhoods then you'll shop at small, local stores instead. One of the main plus-points of twenty-first-century living is that consumers have a choice—so use it wisely.

Here are a few starting tips:

■ Only buy what you really need. Make a shopping list and stick to it to ease the temptation of cut-price offers and BOGOFs (Buy One Get One Free).
■ Cut down on the number of plastic bags you use; bring your own or buy a bag for life.
■ Reduce the amount of packaging you use—plastic production uses around 8 percent of the world's oil supply every year. Buy in bulk or choose loose produce rather than packaged fruits and vegetables.
■ Don't waste a car trip—take a friend.

WHAT TO LOOK OUT FOR

Household products

Many household cleaners, air fresheners, paints, toiletries, and cosmetics contain harmful chemicals and are manufactured in a wasteful and polluting way. Opt for eco-friendly goods instead.

Furniture

New furnishings can contain chemicals that release VOCs into the air, so buy untreated carpets, furniture covers, and cushions in natural materials such as wool, cotton, or hessian. If you're buying wood, look for the FSC logo.

Clothing and textiles

Try to find out how and where your fashion goods are made. Buy organic cotton, secondhand, or from ethical suppliers if you can.

Bottled water

How crazy is it to bottle and ship water around the world and pay up to 10,000 times the price of tap water? Buy bottled water from local sources, or better still use your taps!

Electricals

Buy energy-efficient models, and find out about the manufacturer's environmental

Of course you could simply opt out of consumerism; read how in IDEA 11, *The low-impact consumer.*

Try another idea...

"He who buys what he does not need steals from himself."
ANONYMOUS

Defining idea...

policies. Buy models that have an on/off switch rather than a standby-only option. Greenpeace has a guide to greener mobile phones and PCs. Avoid giant plasma-screen TVs—they use four times the amount of energy of a normal TV.

Palm oil

Palm oil is very versatile and is used in chocolate bars, ice cream, margarine, and other products. But as demand for palm oil plantations increases, so does the threat to the habitats and biodiversity of tropical forests. Only buy from members of the Roundtable on Sustainable Palm Oil (RSPO).

Fish

The world's fish stocks are shrinking alarmingly, thanks to overfishing and pollution. Fish such as tuna, swordfish, cod, salmon, halibut, and some prawns are all endangered. Check out what's best to buy from the Marine Stewardship Council (www.msc.org).

Meat

Avoid intensively farmed meat—chicken and pork in particular—and buy outdoor-reared/free-range and organic when you can.

If this all sounds a bit much, don't worry—just start with one aspect and take it from there. After all, it's better to do something than nothing, so view it as a long-term plan and start off with what fits in best with your lifestyle.

Q   PVC products are everywhere—what's all the fuss about?

A   *Chemicals, such as phthalates, are added to PVC to make it flexible. These have been linked to cancer, and damage to the reproductive system, kidneys, and fetal development. Research shows that children can ingest dangerous chemicals from PVC toys (PVC is now banned from babies' toys).*

During the production of PVC, dioxins (highly toxic chemicals) are created and released. PVC is hard to recycle, so it tends to end up in landfills or incinerators, releasing more pollution. Some governments are already restricting PVC use and many companies such as Nike, IKEA, and The Body Shop aim to eliminate PVC from all their products.

19

Where the wild things are

You may get a buzz from shopping, but every register ring means you're depleting resources. Trade in your plastic bag for a woven basket and forage for wild foods instead.

Switch from shopaholic to cropaholic and scour your neighborhood for berries, nuts, leaves, and fungi. It's all out there...

There's no doubt we're spoiled when it comes to eating food that's strictly out of season, whether it's strawberries in deep winter or cranberries at the height of summer. We're used to having what we want, when we want, all year round.

And yet we have a whole host of wonderful, seasonal produce full of flavor right on our doorstep: the crops that grow wild in hedgerows and fields, on riverbanks and coasts.

It wasn't that long ago in evolutionary terms that we were hunter-gatherers, and while most us have traded in the spear for the plastic card when it comes to feeding the family, I like to think that there's still a lingering echo of the forager in us all. And with nature and the environment on top of the social agenda, foraging and bushcraft have become surprisingly popular in the last few years. There are more wild food experts than you can shake a hazel stick at, and new TV programs, websites, and books reflect the growing interest.

There is nothing more satisfying than spending a day looking out for seasonal goodies such as berries, leaves, seaweed, roots, nuts, and fungi, grown in their natural habitat, not in a chemical soup. It's something the whole family can enjoy, and it gives children especially a chance to spend some quality time away from the computer.

Here's an idea for you...

Learn to love the elder tree. One of the easiest wild foods to gather is its elderberry, which you can pick for nothing along roadsides, public squares, schoolyards, and other open spaces. The deep purple fruits appear in large bunches during the late summer, and aren't particularly pleasant to eat raw, but make a delicious jelly or wine when cooked or fermented. The flowers grow in broad, white, flat clusters, and can also be harvested earlier on in the season and made into a refreshing sparkling drink, either elderflower champagne (mildly alcoholic) or pressé (non-alcoholic).

If you're new to wild foods, your best bet is to go out armed with a good illustrated book, ideally one with recipes—you'll need to know how to prepare those four pounds of fresh nettle leaves.

Obviously, you need to be careful about what you harvest, especially when it comes to berries and fungi. Be absolutely sure before you harvest, and if in doubt, then don't. In no time you'll become an amateur botanist.

Be careful about where you traipse, too. If you're on private property, golf courses, commercial land, sensitive nature reserves, and farmland, ask permission from landowners and farmers before rummaging through hedgerows, even though what you take is unwanted and probably considered a weed.

Another general rule is to only pick the leaves, stems, and fruits of plants, don't dig or pull them up, and never take rare or protected species. In practical terms, the beauty of most edible plants—nettles, dandelions, sorrel, etc.—is that they are very prolific, but there are always exceptions.

Wild food is a wonderful source of extra nutrition but clearly won't fill your stomach all year round. Find out about organic food in IDEA 23, *Go organic.*

Try another idea…

SOME POPULAR WILD FOODS

- Blackberries—versatile and prolific fruits that grow in many open spaces both rural and urban; use them in pies, jams, and jellies.
- Chamomile—a low-growing fragrant plant ideal for a soothing herbal tea.
- Damsons—small, sour plums that make wonderful jam.
- Dandelion leaves—use only the young, spring leaves in salads.
- Garlic mustard—a common hedgerow plant with tasty leaves full of vitamin C that make a great addition to any salad.
- Mushrooms of all kinds—gather them in late summer/early autumn, but make sure you know your fungi!
- Nettles—the young, tender, vitamin C–rich tops can be used like spinach.
- Rosehips—these bright red fruits found on wild roses can be made into a vitamin rich syrup.
- Marsh samphire—found in the summer months along the coast, it looks a bit like cacti. Boiled, it makes a great accompaniment to fish.
- Sloes—gather these small, purple fruits in early autumn and make sloe gin or jelly.
- Wood sorrel—small, sour, clover-like leaves that make good garnishes in spring soups and salads.

"Nature provides a free lunch, but only if we control our appetites."

WILLIAM RUCKELSHAUS

Defining idea…

How did it go?

Q   **I live in the middle of a town. Can I still gather wild foods?**

A   *Of course you can. Parks, sports grounds, municipal gardens, sidewalks, disused railways, and any open, green space can yield rich pickings for the modern hunter-gatherer. You'll get extra satisfaction from knowing that you have plucked them from the urban sprawl. However, it's best to avoid sites very near to main roads.*

Q   **I love the idea of wild foods, but what can I do with them once I find them?**

A   *Since you'll have paid nothing for the stuff you've gathered you can afford to experiment. Use your imagination—you don't need to stick to tried and trusted recipes just because you're taking up ancient practices. Mix your freebies with exotic spices; blend them into a soup; scatter them in salads; devise stylish canapés; or think purée, chutney, oven-dried, jam, deep-fried in batter, or steeped in strong alcohol.*

Q   **Most wild foods seem to be plant-based, but what about animals?**

A   *There is a growing body of people who include roadkill among acceptable, ethical wild food, on the basis that the animal was free, not reared in captivity, and not killed for food. You may want to leave badger, squirrel, and seagull to the professional but, if you do opt for a carnivorous approach, make sure your find has been newly killed (not by you!) and is still warm.*

20

Green gadgets

Anything *eco* is seriously hip these days, and that includes a new breed of "green gadgets" designed to help you save energy and cash.

Some gadgets offer real value for the money, others just look pretty, but it's worth taking a look around to see what's what.

There's a strange paradox going on in the murky world of consumerism. Our appetite for electronics has rocketed over the past few years, with sales totaling billions of dollars worldwide. Yet we're also under massive pressure to reduce energy consumption! It's all a little confusing, but luckily there is a definite move toward smart electronics that only use energy when needed.

Some products really do help save energy or other resources, others are really just eco toys. But maybe even they have a role to play, introducing newcomers to the potential of solar energy for instance, or giving you ideas for recycling newspapers or cans. Increasingly, gadgets have to look the part, too, and have gone from being drab and functional to design-led and eco-chic. New technology and more competition have driven down the price of green gizmos, so you can help save energy without spending a fortune.

Here's an idea for you...

Get an idea of how much electricity your electronics use up on standby by switching off everything else except the stuff you leave on standby and watch your electricity meter spin around for an hour. Take a KW unit reading and cost it from your last bill, then multiply it by twenty-four to see how much your standby appliances use up over just one day. Scary stuff...

SOLAR POWER

Solar has recently gotten sexy. Once a dull-but-worthy technology that simply sat on roofs, solar power has become a handheld tool we can all use. We've seen solar-powered tents, scooters, and LED house numbers, while mundane things like bike and garden lights, flashlights, and radios have been around a while. You can now get small solar-powered devices that run virtually all portable handheld electronic devices, including iPods and cell phones.

There are solar powered wearables, too, such as baseball caps with an integral solar panel and fan, and backpacks that act as a mobile power source, designed to charge your gadgets while on the move.

ELECTRICITY SAVERS

Smart meters, which measure your energy consumption, are pretty much de rigueur for the eco-conscious consumer. Electricity monitors, wireless devices that attach to your electricity meters, give you a real-time display of how much juice you are using wherever you are in the house, plus what this costs and the amount of carbon dioxide it generates. There are even models that look fabulous and change color.

Another way of saving electricity is with a standby cut-off, featuring a switch and two wireless remote control sockets. You plug it into a wall socket and then plug your TV, stereo, computer, etc., into the socket. Just flick the switch when you leave the house and you know you're not wasting energy.

A similar device is a special plug that switches your fridge and freezer off when they don't need power, saving energy of around 20 percent.

For more tips on energy saving measures read IDEA 13, *Warm and cozy*.

Try another idea...

LAUNDRY LOWDOWN

Using eco-balls in your washing machine instead of detergent can save water and energy by removing the need for a second rinse cycle. They produce ionized oxygen that naturally activates the water molecules to create an efficient wash without harsh detergents, using less water and time.

NEWSPAPER RECYCLER

Look out for simple log makers that recycle your newspapers and turn them into bricks to burn on the fire. You need to soak the paper in water, squash it into the log maker, and squeeze down the handles. Remove the brick and leave to dry out.

WIND-UP TECHNOLOGY

Wind-up gadgets, such as the radios invented by Trevor Bayliss, are also enjoying a flush of success, particularly with the debut of the first digital audio broadcasting (DAB) wind-up radio, wind-up flashlights, and wind-up cell phone chargers.

BETTER BATTERIES

We should all be using rechargeable batteries, of course, but on the horizon is a new breed of water-activated, replaceable battery, which produces the same amount of energy as a normal battery, but is made mainly from carbon. These

"Keep your eyes on the sun and you will not see the shadows."
AUSTRALIAN ABORIGINAL PROVERB

Defining idea...

93

batteries are much cheaper (about 10 percent the cost of normal batteries), take less energy to produce, and are nontoxic.

LED LIGHTS

Light Emitting Diode (LED) lightbulbs are the environmentally friendly lights of the future. They last for around 30,000 hours (compared to about 15,000 for a normal low-energy bulb), saving you money and energy. Unlike ordinary incandescent lightbulbs, they don't have a filament that will burn out, and they don't get very hot. Although LED bulbs cost a little more than low-energy bulbs, they have many advantages; they also contain no harmful chemicals (low-energy bulbs can contain mercury), and tend to be smaller and lighter, saving on transport and packaging.

How did it go?

Q   Will I save money with any of these gadgets?

A   *The simple answer is yes—but probably only in the long run. Clearly you have to pay up front for any sort of energy-saving device, but the idea is that over time it will pay for itself. The other side of this technology is that you are reducing your use of fossil fuel, i.e., coal-powered electricity, which is in turn helping reduce greenhouse gases.*

Q   Should I buy now or wait for technology to improve?

A   *Technology is advancing all the time and as it gets more sophisticated the prices of these gadgets are bound to drop. If you want an all-singing, all-dancing device then it is probably better to wait and see if the price does go down. But for the basics, there's no time like the present, as you can start saving energy and resources now.*

21

Clothes care

By all means stay fresh, but laundering and ironing your clothing with the minimum use of chemicals and energy is the twenty-first-century way to go.

Are you super fussy when it comes to clothes care? If the answer's yes, you could also be using up valuable resources.

We may as well be back in the days when you boiled your whites in a massive pan on the stove—it always surprises me how many people routinely wash their laundry at very high temperatures. What a waste of electricity! It shortens the life of fabric, too.

Modern, highly efficient detergents are designed so you can usually reduce the temperature of your wash to around 86 degrees F without compromising cleanliness, meaning you use a whopping 40 percent less electricity. You can get away with a shorter wash, too.

Wait until you've got a full load before using your washing machine—using the "half load" program does not save you half the energy, water, or detergent—and use the economy program where possible. Combine clothes with the same wash symbol, but if you have to machine wash mixed loads, put them through the most delicate cycle on their labels.

Here's an idea for you... **Love the idea of never having to buy detergent again? Then suspend your skepticism and try laundry balls. These little plastic reusable spheres are used in place of soap, meaning you use less water and less electricity as you bypass the rinse cycle. They work by producing ionized oxygen that naturally activates the water molecules. The balls soften the water so no fabric softener is needed and also minimize color fading. If your clothes are very stained, you can add a little eco-detergent. You can order them online from most green suppliers, and each pack of three should last for 1,000 washes.**

BE KIND TO YOUR WASHING MACHINE

Help prolong the life of your washing machine and keep it working efficiently.

- Go through all the pockets to check for pens, coins, tissues, etc.—they won't do your machine or wash any favors.
- Before loading, shake items out, and load one at a time to reduce tangling—small items first, then large. Don't overfill it.
- Clean your washing machine occasionally by clearing out filters and running it empty on a hot cycle with a little white vinegar in the detergent compartment to clear soap deposits.
- Buy refill packs of detergents and fabric softeners. Use correct dosages; don't guess.
- Use eco-friendly laundry products.

USING A TUMBLE DRYER

It's obviously more environmentally friendly to dry laundry outside rather than tumble dry it, but if you must:

- Spin dry clothes first unless the label advises not to.
- Don't run a tumble dryer too long because this wastes energy and overdries the clothes, which makes ironing more difficult.

- Help it work efficiently by leaving plenty of space for clothes to move around.

For more ideas on keeping pristine but saving resources, try IDEA 6, *Clean but green*.

Try another idea…

IRONING AND DRYING CLOTHES

- Keep ironing to a minimum by hanging up or folding clothes as soon as they come out of the tumble dryer.
- Iron items that need the coolest setting first, and work up to the hottest setting. Iron in loads, as irons use a lot of electricity heating up.
- Use shiny board covers to reflect heat back onto the clothes and improve efficiency, or place aluminum foil underneath.

DRY-CLEANING

Dry-cleaning has to be one of the most environmentally unsound ways of laundering clothes. The strong smell of chemicals as you step into your local shop is a dead giveaway, and the plastic cover and disposable hanger just add to its sins. The solvent used by the vast majority of cleaners is tetrachloroethylene, also known as perchloroethylene, or perc, the latest in a long line of chemicals used to clean delicate textiles.

A number of cleaning firms are now looking for safer alternatives, one being global company GreenEarth, which uses relatively harmless liquid silicon. But if your local dry cleaner is less than green, it's best to simply reduce the amount of "dry-clean only" clothing you buy. Some items can, with care, be hand washed.

"The necessity of practicing economy should be evident to everyone."

ISABELLA BEETON

Defining idea…

97

Q **I dry-clean clothes because it keeps moths away. Any ideas on natural repellents?**

A *Moths thrive in dust and dirt, so before you store clothes or bedding, clean them and air them well. Clean out wardrobes, cupboards, and drawers regularly. Natural moth deterrents include dried citrus peel, eucalyptus oil, cloves, and lavender sachets. Brush and dust dark cupboards regularly and then sprinkle with a few drops of cedarwood oil. Alternatively, hang up bags containing a mixture of lavender and pennywort.*

Q **Many of my clothes are hand wash only. How can I keep them clean using natural materials?**

A *Try biodegradable soap flakes or liquid made from natural vegetable oils, but dissolve them thoroughly first. Keep the water no more than tepid and use cold water for rinsing; splash a little vinegar into the final rinse to remove all the suds. Brighten up yellowing cotton items by soaking them in hot water with a cupful of lemon juice, or a pinch of borax or bicarbonate of soda.*

Q **I keep reading about soap nuts—what are they?**

A *The nut is the dried fruit of the rittha tree, native to India and Nepal. When the shells of the soap nut come in to contact with water, saponin is released and suds are produced. They have been used for centuries as a washing detergent, multi-surface cleaner, and a shampoo. Organic and biodegradable, soap nuts are also sustainable and renewable, and their harvest supplements the income of many families in the region. You can buy them online and from eco-stores.*

22

Let's step outside

When it comes to being green, you need to be squeaky clean both inside and out!

Beauty may come from within, but when it comes to being green, what's on the outside counts, too. Take a stroll around your home—could you be doing better?

Because we spend around 90 percent of our time indoors, it's all too easy to focus on the inside of your home when it comes to green issues. But there are certainly steps you can take all around your home to improve its eco-status—summer and winter alike.

DECKS, FENCES, AND FURNITURE

Think reclaimed timber when it comes to outdoor hardware. Old wood is well seasoned, affordable, and doesn't plunder resources. Use it for fences, gates, and decking. Old railway sleepers can be bought cheaply and are great for creating beds or sectioning off parts of the garden. Recycled plastic decking looks good and is easy to maintain, and garden furniture is now available in this recycled material, too.

If you want new wood, look out for the Forest Stewardship Council (FSC) logo to be sure it is from a sustainable source. You could also cultivate your own border—

Sometimes it pays to be a neighborhood snoop. Next time there is settled snow or frost, take a look at the roof of your home. If the snow or frost there is melting faster than the guy next door's, it's because your insulation isn't doing its job. Heat from inside your home is escaping upward, causing the icy covering to melt. Up to 25 percent of heat is lost through un-insulated roofs, so having the recommended 11 inches of insulation in the attic should help conserve energy, keep your house warmer, and result in a drop in your annual fuel bill.

plant hedgerows and wait for your fence to grow!

ROOFING

Retiling the roof? Investigate using recycled plastic slate-effect tiles. They're totally convincing even on close inspection but won't crack and age like natural slate. Or try them as cladding material for your exterior walls.

WATER BUTTS

This season's gardening must-have, a water butt, collects rainwater runoff from the gutters; essential in times of drought for watering and car washing.

GARAGE

Get into the habit of cleaning out the garage every now and then, safely disposing of hazardous materials such as old paints, thinners, adhesives, car oil, methylated spirits, pool chemicals, and car batteries. Recycle what you can and seek advice from your local authority on how to dispose of the rest.

PATIO HEATERS

With product names like Arizona and Sahara Big Burn, need I say more? Patio heaters are the bad boys of the eco-movement, kicking out the emissions of a speeding truck and heating up the atmosphere without so much as a pane of glass between them and the ozone layer. Put on a jacket or go indoors!

BARBECUES

Ah, the tantalizing scent of charcoal and freshly barbecued food, the clink of glasses, and the soft air of a warm summer's evening—nothing beats a good barbecue. But your Sunday afternoon meat fest could be giving off more than a curl of wood smoke. If you're a charcoal briquette fan, hold that burger! These briquettes release carbon monoxide, particulates, and harmful volatile organic compounds (VOCs) thanks to their chemical additives. Propane, also called liquid petroleum gas, or LPG, burns more cleanly than charcoal briquettes, meaning less localized pollution, but it is still a fossil fuel and a CO_2 baddie.

Real grill jockeys insist on natural wood charcoal, luckily also the most environmentally friendly, too. Charcoal is carbon neutral, but some of the charcoal we burn each year is sourced from vulnerable tropical forests. The best option for a green barbie is charcoal from producers who use traditional and sustainable methods. And don't forget to compost the charcoal ash.

LIGHTING

There's a growing trend for homes to be brilliantly floodlit all night. This is complete waste of electricity, irritating to neighbors, and disruptive to wildlife. If you install security lighting, make it movement sensitive and timed to go off after a short while. Look out for solar lighting for gardens and sheds, and you can also get solar-powered water features, too.

The garden's green, but not necessarily in all senses of the word. Read up on natural ways to grow in IDEA 31, *Garden green*.

Try another idea...

"What is the use of a house if you haven't got a tolerable planet to put it on?"
HENRY DAVID THOREAU, writer and philosopher

Defining idea...

How did
it go? **Q   Anything I can do to "green" the outside of my home without spending any money?**

A   *Sometimes there's nothing wrong in being a Luddite. The suburbs are abuzz with hi-tech garden tools—gas- and electricity-powered mowers, cutters, blowers, trimmers, pressure washers, vacuums, barbecues, and shredders, which may take the sweat out of gardening but don't exactly help your carbon footprint. They all use unnecessary energy—which you end up paying for—and cause noise pollution as well. So why not pitch in with a good old-fashioned broom, shears, or rake? If you must tool up, organize a neighborhood swap shop and pool resources.*

Q   My drains are always getting blocked. Any ideas for nontoxic maintenance?

A   *One of the worst things you can do when your drain gets blocked is to slosh corrosive chemical cleaner down it, which will then enter the waterways. Turn to your plunger instead, or invest in a pack of rods for home use. Biological cleaners with natural enzymes are another option. Or try prevention: a weekly sluice with bicarbonate of soda and cheap vinegar, then a flush with boiling water. Assuming there is no underlying problem, are you perhaps using your drains as a trash bin? Beware of solids— condoms, cotton balls, cooking fats, diapers, and all kinds of sanitary protection should be wrapped or bagged and thrown away, not flushed.*

23

Go organic

Who would choose a food stuffed full of chemicals over one that is clean and green?

No longer the preserve of hippies and vegans, organic food is becoming more affordable and easily available.

When governments start advising you to cut the top and tail off of carrots to get rid of the most toxic pesticides (which is what happened in the UK), you know it's time to switch to organic. Sure, some people insist that there are no health benefits to organic produce, but personally I'd rather not wait around to find out when the stores are positively bulging with delicious chemical-free produce.

Organic food is also softer on the environment than factory-farmed produce and should offer animals kinder living conditions.

To be organic, the food must have been produced on an organic farm, which is free of any chemical fertilizer or pesticides. Animals on organic farms must be kept and slaughtered in a humane manner.

When you look at a product that claims to be organic, in most cases you will see the symbol of an organic agency, for example the Soil Association (www.soilassociation.org).

Here's an idea for you...

Yes, that organic price tag can hurt! Naturally produced food can be pricey, and you may well balk at shelling out that extra cash. If cost is an issue, jot down a list of the main five or six foods that you eat and see whether you can afford to make these into your organic must-haves. Bulky basics might include bread, potatoes, milk, meat, eggs, root vegetables, salads, and cereals that could have a real impact on your diet, whereas smaller items such as garlic, dips, or herbs probably won't make a huge difference whether grown organically or not.

DELIVERY SERVICES

It always gives me a little thrill when my weekly box arrives, a colorful mass of the freshest possible produce, mud still clinging to wherever it's supposed to cling! It really is the easiest way to try out organics. A selection of seasonal produce is delivered to you from an organic farm, normally weekly. Most plans offer a range of boxes, each with a set selection of farm produce, but you can often mix and match. You usually also have the option of organic extras such as cheese, honey, preserves, meat, and eggs.

Most of the year you get a good variety, but there are a couple of lean months when not much is growing, and then some services beef up the contents with imported goods.

Before you commit, look into the origins of the service's produce as well as compare prices. In addition to being accredited by an organic agency, ideally it will be as near to you as possible to reduce the food miles, and should of course recycle all the cardboard boxes it uses.

FARMERS' MARKETS

Farmers' markets in parking lots, fields, halls, or other open spaces are becoming increasingly popular, and you can see why. As well as giving you the chance to wander around looking—and tasting—different kinds of foodstuffs, they offer you the chance to chat with the producer and learn about their growing or manufacturing methods. Expect to find good quality meat, eggs, dairy produce, cakes, preserves, fruit, vegetables, puddings, honey, and more.

Who said there was no such thing as a free lunch? Forage around in IDEA 19, *Where the wild things are.*

Try another idea...

Keep an eye on whether food is organic or not by looking out for accreditation, perhaps in the form of a certificate on their stall. If they are in the process of becoming organic, ask how they are going about it.

SUPERMARKETS

Supermarkets have undergone a sea change in the last couple of years, and now most are bending over backward to offer a good range of organic foodstuffs. Prices still remain on the high side, but stores tend to say they are simply reflecting the extra costs needed to produce organic food and that profit margins are the same as for all their other food.

WINE

Bacchus, the ancient god of wine, would surely nod in approval were he to see the amount of vino we quaff today. But he perhaps would have shaken his head over some of its production methods and additives.

"Modern man no longer regards Nature as in any sense divine."

ALDOUS HUXLEY

Defining idea...

Many of the world's vineyards are now highly industrialized and use pesticides like they are going out of fashion. There have been mutterings about exploitative immigrant labor, too.

And when wine is coming from another continent, we have to wonder just how sustainable it is to ship a heavy liquid in glass across vast oceans. Perhaps one answer is to buy organic wine from as near as possible. Or you could try a fair-trade wine, beer, or spirit. Or make your own, of course!

How did it go?

Q   I eat mainly organic, well-sourced food at home but how can I continue when I'm out and about?

A   *More and more restaurants are sourcing locally produced organic food, which they usually can't wait to trumpet on their menus, so it should be pretty easy to see which offerings fall into that category. There is also a new breed of restaurant where everything is run along ethical lines, including staff wages and conditions, sourcing, recycling, and even wormeries! If you're prepared to travel, some working organic farms run excellent restaurants and cafés and are happy to show you around, too.*

24

Homemade goodies

Preparing your own preserves, pickles, cordials, and dried herbs maximizes seasonal produce and saves you cash.

You don't have to buy out-of-season produce that's traveled thousands of miles—just preserve what you can when it's harvest time.

It may seem like a lot of hard work to pick, wash, prepare, and cook foods to turn them into preserves when you can simply run down to the store and buy the equivalent in a jar.

But there's a simple pleasure in producing your own range of foodstuffs, and especially so when you're using the season's finest. With exotic produce on demand at supermarkets, we are out of touch with the smells and sights of the seasonal. There's nothing like the fruity aroma of jam-making in late summer, the scent of simmering winter berries and spices at Christmas, or the sharp tang of an autumn pickling session.

Making your own preserves brings you back in touch with a food's origins, and is really just another way of enjoying local, seasonal produce. And of course you are fully in control of what goes in—no artificial additives, preservatives, or sweeteners.

Here's an idea for you... **Get into the habit of keeping any jars with a screw lid rather than spending a small fortune on store-bought preserving glassware. Homemade preserves, pickles, chutneys, and cordials look fabulously colorful when you line them up in your cupboard, and even better when stored in a variety of attractive containers. You can also source pretty period jars from antiques markets, yard sales, and charities. They need to be washed well and sterilized with boiling water or in a low oven, and ideally made airtight with greaseproof paper discs or rubber seals that you can buy separately from department or hardware stores.**

You can use organic ingredients (including fair-trade sugar, of course!), perhaps grown in your own garden or allotment or just plucked from the hedgerows that morning. They make fantastic gifts, too.

JAMS AND JELLIES

A traditional jam is made by cooking whole or cut fruit with sugar, while a jelly is made by cooking the juice of the fruit with sugar.

Always use fruit that's in peak condition, preferably slightly underripe, when the pectin (setting agent) content will be at its highest. Don't use overripe or damaged fruit, as the jam won't turn out as well.

CHUTNEYS AND PICKLES

In chutneys, vinegar rather than sugar is the main preserving agent and is cooked with vegetables, orchard fruits, or other fruits such as peaches, bananas, mangoes, and apricots.

Pickles are normally made with vegetables that are preserved whole or in large pieces in vinegar flavored with spices. They are normally pickled raw to preserve their crunchy texture.

SUN- OR OVEN-DRIED FRUITS AND VEGETABLES

Drying produce either in a very low oven or in the sun is a good method of preserving certain types of fruits and vegetables including tomatoes, peppers, and apples. The flavor is intensified—compare the sweet and chewy semi-dried tomato to a fresh one, or the intense flavor of dried apricots compared to the rather bland fresh fruit you buy off the shelves. Dried preserves can be added to salads, soups, or casseroles, or eaten as a snack or a starter.

If the idea of getting in touch with your inner squirrel appeals, learn about easy fruits and veggies to grow at home in IDEA 34, *Grow your own*.

Try another idea...

INFUSED OILS

Grow your own chilis, garlic, and herbs, add them to a favorite oil such as olive or groundnut and allow them to infuse for a couple of weeks. Elegantly presented in a nice recycled bottle, these make ecologically sound gifts, too.

WINES, CORDIALS, AND SPIRITS

You can make your own organic, deep-hued wines and cordials from soft fruits such as blackcurrants, sloes, elderberries, and raspberries. If you prefer something a little stronger, add fruits to strong spirits—rum, brandy, or gin—and allow the colors and flavors to infuse for a few weeks.

DRIED HERBS

You can grow your own supply of organic herbs in a pot, window box, or garden, and dry them before they die off. Pick what you can, wash them gently, and then hang them upside down

"In the early autumn, plums of various kinds are to be bottled and preserved, and jams and jellies made."
ISABELLA BEETON

Defining idea...

in decorative bunches. Store dried herbs in airtight containers, preferably not plastic, away from sunlight, and use them within a year.

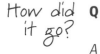

Q **Making preserves sounds like a lot of effort. Is it worth it?**

A *You may not think it's worth it for just one jar, but make them in bulk and you'll reap the rewards all year round. If you grow your own, you're bound to get a bumper crop at some point, or failing that, ask gardening friends or neighbors (reward them with a pot of the finished product). Scour markets at the end of the day for bargains, and collect jars whenever you can. Dressed up with fancy labels and ribbons, preserves also make fantastic gifts.*

Q **There is only so much apple jelly I can take. How else can I preserve the crop I get each year from my garden?**

A *Slow drying apples is a good way of making them last. Dried apple can be added to cereals or cakes or eaten on its own as a healthy snack. Try peeling, coring, and cutting apples into rings and hanging them on strings somewhere very warm, or drying them in a very low oven.*

Q **How long can I safely keep homemade jams or chutneys for?**

A *You should be able to enjoy the fruits of your labor for up to a year, so long as they are stored in a cool, dry place and well sealed, and you have sterilized the jars properly first.*

25

First aid, naturally

Why spend a fortune on synthetic medicines when there are perfectly acceptable natural alternatives available?

Ditch the chemical-based antibacterial spray and start a collection of tried and trusted natural remedies.

Hard to believe, but dumped over-the-counter (OTC) medicines form a quite substantial part of hazardous waste in landfill sites. Small in themselves, packets, jars, and tubes of OTCs nevertheless combine to form thousands of tons of chemical-leaching landfill globally.

While I wouldn't suggest swapping important drugs for herbs or oils, there is surely a place for natural remedies in the medicine cabinet for minor conditions. Many of them can provide considerable relief, most are nontoxic and often suitable for children (although not always for pregnant or breast-feeding women) but always check the label first and with your doctor if you are on any medication.

■ **Aloe vera**—Best used in gel form, this plant-based remedy is good for all kinds of minor wounds and burns, including sunburns.
■ **Arnica**—Used for bruises, sprains, and sore muscles, this remedy is available in a cream or ointment, or can be given as a compress.

- **Calendula**—This herb is anti-inflammatory, astringent, and antiseptic. You can find it in salve form, often in combination with comfrey and other healing herbs. Use it for cuts, scrapes, rashes, burns, bruises, strains, and sprains.
- **Chamomile**—A pleasant-smelling herb used as an anti-inflammatory as well as a digestive aid, and good for diaper rash or other rashes.
- **Eucalyptus essential oil**—A potent antibiotic and antiviral, eucalyptus is good for treating colds and sinus infections when used as a steam inhalation.
- **Fennel**—Fennel oil, especially combined with chamomile, is soothing to an upset stomach. Put a few drops in water to take when tummyaches strike (add a few drops of clove, caraway, or anise oil for a pleasing taste), or massage the stomach with chamomile and fennel in a carrier oil.
- **Ginger capsules, tea bags, and crystallized ginger**—The antispasmodic and gas-relieving properties of ginger soothe digestive upsets. Ginger also has been shown to relieve motion sickness.
- **Goldenseal capsules or powder**—A powerful antimicrobial, goldenseal is effective against a variety of microorganisms that cause traveler's diarrhea. The powder has antiseptic properties and can be sprinkled onto cuts or wounds to stop bleeding.
- **Grindelia tincture or spray**—Grindelia contains resins and tannins that help to relieve the pain and itching of plant rashes. It's available as a tincture and also as a spray.

Here's an idea for you...

You don't need to clear out your local health store's shelves to make up your own natural first-aid kit. Start with just one or two tried and trusted basics such as tea tree and lavender oil, arnica, witch hazel, and aloe vera, building it up from there. Try out remedies on yourself and your family—most of them are harmless as long as you follow the instructions—to see which produce the best results. It's important that you actually enjoy using the product; research shows that the placebo effect works alongside the medicinal one to produce a stronger healing experience.

- **Lavender essential oil**—Lavender oil offers relief for the sting or itch of insect bites, minor burns, and bruises. Use lavender oil undiluted on the skin, or put a few drops in a lukewarm bath.

- **Papaya**—This tropical fruit contains the enzyme papain, which researchers say aids digestion by helping your body break down proteins. Available as chewable papaya tablets, or you can enjoy unsweetened papaya juice or a wedge of fresh papaya.

- **Peppermint essential oil and tea bags**—A high concentration of menthol means that peppermint soothes an upset stomach, clears sinuses, and curbs itching from insect bites.

- **St. John's wort**—Herbal St. John's wort has anti-inflammatory properties and can be used topically on minor wounds and burns, or blended with oil to massage aching muscles.

- **Senna**—Most herbal laxative teas rely on senna, often combined with herbs such as cinnamon, fennel, licorice, and ginger to mask its bitter taste.

- **Tea tree essential oil**—Tea tree has potent antifungal and antiseptic properties, making it a useful remedy for athlete's foot, minor wounds, insect repellent, and head lice—though it can cause rashes on sensitive skin.

- **Tiger Balm**—To treat muscle cramps and headaches, rub this salve on the affected muscle or temples, avoiding the eyes.

- **Valerian tincture**—The sedative properties of valerian make it useful for relieving anxiety, insomnia, and tension.

- **Witch hazel extract**—Distilled witch hazel has mild astringent, antiseptic, and anti-inflammatory properties, so it's handy for insect bites and skin irritations.

Love the idea of going back to old-fashioned, nontoxic household remedies? Check out more in IDEA 6, *Clean but green*.

Try another idea...

"If I'd known I was going to live so long, I'd have taken better care of myself."

LEON ELDRED, humorist

Defining idea...

113

Q **I don't buy into all this alternative stuff. How do I know these natural treatments work?**

A *Before you condemn them out of hand, bear in mind that around 60 percent of over-the-counter medicines are based on natural ingredients according to the US Food and Drug Administration! Why not give just one of them a try? Choose the one that appeals to you the most, that smells the nicest, or is the cheapest!*

Q **I like the idea of using natural remedies but are they safe for my children?**

A *Many of the natural herbs and oils in common use are gentle enough to be safe for children, and some have a pleasant taste that should appeal to younger patients. However, others, such as tea tree, eucalyptus, and witch hazel must not be swallowed. Check the label first. Like any medicine, natural remedies should be kept out of reach of little hands, in a high or locked cupboard.*

Q **How long do natural remedies last?**

A *Kept in a cool, dark, dry place, most should last for at least a year. In the case of essential oils, they should come in a dark glass bottle to offer extra protection against light.*

26

Low-power dressing

Green is definitely the new black: Highly creative eco-fashion is flying off the shelves and into wardrobes all over the world.

If it's eco, it's in. More and more fashion brands are jumping on the ethical bandwagon, so there's plenty of choice out there.

If you stand back and examine your wardrobe, you're more likely to be fretting over its shortcomings as a fashion statement than as an eco-product.

But behind every garment is a story, and often it's not a good one. Many clothes are made from synthetic materials such as nylon and polyester, which come from highly polluting petrochemicals whose manufacture contributes to climate change. They are also non-biodegradable, which means they are difficult to dispose of.

Natural fibers aren't all squeaky clean, either. Cotton uses more pesticide per plant than almost any other crop, causing damage to the environment and the people who farm it. The chemicals used to grow or treat cotton remain in the fabric and are released during the lifetime of the garments so they affect people wearing clothes, too.

Here's an idea for you... **Keep tabs on your wardrobe so you don't become a wasteful hoarder. If you haven't worn something for a year, out it should go! Your idea of a designer disaster could be someone else's dress to-die-for, so why not get together with a few friends and host a clothes swap party? If each guest brings along a bag full of wearable but unwanted clothes, chances are between you you'll be able to swap quite a few outfits over a glass of wine or two. Any remaining items can be donated to charity.**

In many parts of the world, garments are dyed or bleached using chemicals that affect workers and flow into sewers and rivers, damaging local ecosystems.

Virtually all polycotton plus all "easy-care" and "crease-resistant" cotton are treated with the toxic chemical formaldehyde.

But the fashion industry, or parts of it, is one step ahead, and is now turning its attention to producing a new breed of environmentally friendly clothing, or eco-fashion. Eco-fashion is manufactured using low carbon, nontoxic processes, and includes organic clothing, recycled textiles, and materials such as plastic drink bottles. Yes, it does come with a higher price tag, but wouldn't you rather pay a little more knowing that workers aren't being exploited and the planet trashed?

ORGANICS

Organic fashion, where clothes that have been made with a minimum use of chemicals, does the minimum damage to the environment. For instance, organic cotton is grown without the use of chemical pesticides and insecticides, and organic cotton garments are often also free from chlorine bleaches and synthetic dyes.

Hemp needs few or no agrichemicals to grow, and at the same time it binds and enriches the soil with its deep roots.

Linen is made from flax, another traditional fiber crop that needs few chemical fertilizers, and less pesticide than cotton.

Organic wool is produced using sustainable farming practices and without toxic sheep dips.

Bamboo has recently been developed as a clothing fiber, which is great for eco-fashion as it's highly sustainable and produces clothing that is soft, breathable, and fast-drying.

Look after your clothes and they'll look after you, but keep it green in IDEA 21, Clothes care.

Try another idea...

FAIR TRADE AND FASHION

You can find fair-trade products by looking out for the Fair Trade Certified logo, which guarantees that that product has been made in line with standards as set out by TransFair USA (www.transfairusa.org).

RECYCLING

Take old clothing to charity or recycling points, support fashion brands, charities, and businesses that use secondhand and recycled products, or customize your own clothing to extend its life.

"Fashion passes, style remains."

COCO CHANEL

Defining idea...

JEWELRY

Jewelry is not exempt from the ethical minefield, as anyone who has seen the film *Blood Diamond* will know. In fact, diamonds have gone from being a girl's best friend to being a downright eco-enemy, linked to arms funding in Africa, child slave labor in India, and huge environmental damage. The ethically minded are now only buying certified diamonds, or shunning diamonds in favor of semi-precious stones such as agate, jasper, and carnelian. Gold has a tarnished image, too, for similar reasons. Buy from reputable sources, ask to see certification, and think about buying recycled precious metals.

Q **Are there any organizations that can give me more information about ethical fashion?**

How did it go?

A *There are lots. Go to www.naturalmatters.net for a directory of eco-clothing makers. Clean Clothes Campaign (www.cleanclothes.org) is an international campaign focused on improving working conditions in the garment and sportswear industries. It has links to other bodies that are working to produce better conditions for fashion industry workers worldwide. Fairtrade Labelling Organizations International (www.fairtrade.net) is an association of twenty labeling initiatives that promote and market the Fair Trade Certification Mark globally.*

Q **How can I find out where and how a garment was made?**

A *If it's not on the label, go online—many large retail chains, manufacturers, and designers have information about sourcing policies and social responsibility on their websites. If you can't get the information you want that way, ask the store to tell you where it was made and whether the person making it was paid fairly. You may not get a very helpful or knowledgeable response, but if stores are getting lots of similar questions, they will have to provide answers eventually.*

Q **Is there any use for my old shoes?**

A *Shoes that look down at the heel to you would be more than welcome to someone who may not own any others. Several charities run initiatives to collect secondhand shoes and send them to AIDS-torn countries in Africa, for example, or they may pass them on to local homeless people. Charities like Oxfam can sell them through their shops, too, if they're in reasonable condition. Give them a good cleaning first, though!*

27

Your body, your skin

When is natural not natural? When it's a faux "eco" beauty product that is stuffed full of the usual chemicals.

Pamper yourself by all means, but could your beauty products be doing you—and the planet—more harm than good?

Like many other industries, the world of beauty is undergoing something of a revolution, with manufacturers racing to get new organic or "ethical" products onto the shelves as fast as they can. Greater consumer savvy about ingredients and sourcing has driven some brands to rethink their whole ethos right down to the packaging they come in and their involvement with the communities they source from.

And perhaps it's just as well.

The average Western bathroom cabinet is a veritable pharmacopeia of shampoo, soap, mouthwash, toothpaste, shaving gels, and hygiene products. These products contain a wide variety of chemical substances, the safety of which remains questionable. There are over 1000 chemicals currently available to manufacturers of cosmetics and toiletries suspected to have harmful effects. Some of these survive the journey through sewage works into the sea.

Our skin soaks up 60 percent of what we put on it, which ultimately can end up traveling throughout our entire systems. The term "natural" is now highly

If you have a hoard of old cosmetics and toiletries lurking in your makeup bag, chuck them out! Changing legislation is slowly nudging out the most harmful chemicals (although many remain), but the older a product the more likely it is to contain potentially damaging substances that can be absorbed through the skin. Look out especially for synthetic fragrances or musks, dental products containing Triclosan, and permanent hair dyes that carry warnings of possible allergic reactions. Switch to natural products, for example the WWF's range of gentle toiletries and cosmetics, that have the added benefit of not being tested on animals or containing animal materials.

dubious—a product has to have only 1 percent natural ingredients to earn this moniker!

There are a number of genuinely natural products on the market. The best ones will provide a list of ingredients, and most of these ingredients will have familiar names. (Natural soaps, for instance, will contain coconut, corn, soy, or olive oil.)

Look out for the word "organic" instead, and especially for logos such as the Soil Association's, which will guarantee 95 percent organic contents.

There are other ways to be ethical. Take a look at the way the manufacturer runs its company. Aside from what it puts into its products, it should have a responsible attitude toward the environment. Ask about company policies on chemical usage, recycling, employment, and health and safety. Support companies whose policies you agree with.

Some of the best companies run initiatives in developing countries, too, although that doesn't necessarily mean that their products don't still contain chemicals such as preservatives. (For instance, The Body Shop products are based on ingredients from natural sources wherever possible, but may contain synthetic chemicals where they are needed, e.g., for safety or where no suitable natural alternatives exist.) The Body Shop sources cocoa butter for its moisturizers from the Kuapa Kokoo cooperative in Ghana. As well as its non-animal testing policy, The Body Shop is committed to environmental protection and has a large community trade strategy.

Look good and feel good inside by wearing your ethics on your back in IDEA 26, *Low-power dressing*.

Try another idea...

Aveda, another ethical company, makes use of wind power, which offsets 100 percent of the electricity used by its main manufacturing facility. Aveda has raised more than $6 million for environmental causes since 1999 through its Earth Month campaigns.

Other things you can do:

- Wear less makeup! Try going a day without makeup and see whether people even notice.
- Buy cosmetic and beauty products that are simply formulated and as ecologically sound as possible.
- Try to avoid synthetic fragrances and perfumes, and opt for diluted essential oils instead.
- Don't believe all the hype — watch out for "greenwash" (bogus or inflated environmental claims) and pseudoscientific claims. Words like "natural," "environmentally sound," or "safe" often can't be substantiated. Read the small print first, and look out for specific information that backs up claims and certification from recognized bodies.
- Avoid products in unnecessary packaging.
- Avoid PVC packaging, as it's hard to recycle and toxic to manufacture. PVC is signaled by a recycling triangle with a 3 in the middle of it.

"If you think you're too small to have an impact, try going to bed with a mosquito in the room."

ANITA RODDICK

Defining idea...

123

How did it go?

Q   **Many natural and organic products are expensive. Are there any cheaper options?**

A   *Try making your own! That way you have complete control over what's inside, and you can source the best quality organic ingredients at the best prices by shopping around or buying online. For instance, you could use coconut, almond, jojoba, avocado, and wheat-germ oils as hair conditioner, mixed with an essential oil such as lavender or rosemary for fragrance. Natural henna is a great smoother, too. Make a face mask with oatmeal, and moisturizers from cocoa butter and sesame, almond, or vitamin E oils, perhaps mixed with rosewater or honey.*

Q   **I'd like to be ethical in more ways than one—how can I tell if toiletries have been tested on animals?**

A   *All kinds of products and ingredients are tested on animals, and labeling can be misleading—while an end product may not have been tested, one of its ingredients may have. The EU ban on animal testing for cosmetics begins in 2009, but countries like the United States and Japan are far from ending testing, and products are likely to have been tested on animals unless it states otherwise. Look for products approved under The Humane Cosmetics Standard (HCS), the world's only international overseer for cruelty-free beauty products.*

Q   **How can I tell if my toiletries contain toxic chemicals?**

A   *You can get more information from organizations such as the Environmental Working Group (www.ewg.org), which lists potentially harmful chemicals and their effects.*

28

A change of sport?

Whether you're on the slopes, in the waves, behind the wheel, or on the green, have you thought about the environmental impact your sport of choice might have?

It's a no-brainer: Some of the most enjoyable and inclusive sports are clean, green, and absolutely free!

The message is coming across loud and clear: We should all be playing sports, and lots of them. Well, that's indisputable, but there's no getting away from the fact that some resource-hungry sports use up large tracts of land and water, disturb wildlife, or throw harmful emissions into the air.

Skiing, for one, has a huge impact on the planet. Mountains are torn apart to open up the wide runs favored by skiers, and roads are bulldozed into the hills. Customers fly or drive in, often in large SUVs. Increasingly the snow is less than satisfactory, and has to be created using chemicals and electricity and then sculpted into shape by diesel-hungry machines. Energy is used in huge quantities to carry skiers up slopes, only for them to slide back down again!

Some resorts are waking up to the problems, and trying to manage the slopes in a more sustainable fashion. For instance, the Colorado resorts of Aspen and Vail

Here's an idea for you...

Walking is one environmentally friendly sport you could take up today. You don't need any special equipment apart from a good pair of shoes, or any preparation, as you can go at your own pace. Walking is low impact in all senses: it uses minimal resources, doesn't cost a penny, and is gentle enough to suit all abilities. It's good for your heart, lungs, muscles, and bone growth, and your feeling of well-being. People who walk regularly have reduced mortality rates, and up to half the risk of cardiovascular disease. Walkers are less anxious, sleep well, and have better body weight control. Experts recommend thirty minutes of brisk walking daily.

have introduced measures such as electricity offsetting, wind turbines, vehicles powered by biodiesel, and careful water management.

In France, Courchevel, Méribel, and Belleville have announced a joint eco-initiative under the banner "Three Valleys Go Green." And Werfenweng, a village in Austria, now boasts electric cars and solar panels.

Of course it's not just skiing that's affecting the planet. Anything with an engine—motor racing, Jet Skiing, dirtbike riding, power boating—is less than green, not to mention noisy. Golf, swallowing up large areas of countryside, thousands of gallons of water, and using all sorts of chemicals to keep its green green, is one of the biggest culprits, especially in the parched regions of Portugal and Spain where golfing resorts have been accused of taking more than their fair share of the local water supply.

Even sports such as football and baseball that are inherently harmless cause major environmental effects, thanks to the transport of spectators, the litter they produce, and the power required for the stadiums.

Defining idea...

"I have two doctors, my left leg and my right."
GEORGE TREVELYAN

Gyms are pretty greedy, too. Think of the huge amounts of energy needed to heat the halls and pools, keep all those exercise machines turning, refrigerate the drink machines, and power the banks of TVs; the only thing that gets recycled is the air!

Of course there are many sports that don't eat up land, water, or blast emissions into the atmosphere unless practiced in a huge power-hungry stadium: cycling, walking, yoga, pilates, horse riding, martial arts, swimming in the sea, rivers or lakes, jogging, and many team sports.

But the ultimate in sustainable could be green gyms, eco-friendly, cheaper alternatives to traditional health clubs. Members "work out" outdoors, in the countryside or other open spaces, while all that energy goes to some use in conservation activities, such as planting trees, dry-stone walling, or creating school nature areas. No special experience or gear is required. And best of all—unlike your local gym—it's free.

Whatever sport you take up, you can make it greener by asking for eco-friendly equipment, lobbying any clubs you are a member of to go low carbon, and buying products made from recycled or sustainable materials. Surfboards, for instance, are traditionally made from poly foam, fiberglass, and petroleum-derived resins, but new models use less harmful eco foam, balsa wood, plant-based materials, hemp cloth, and bio-resin. And many sport clothes are now made from organic cotton or bamboo, which is sustainable, dries quickly, and is both soft and lightweight.

If you've got your head around eco-sport, you may be ready for eco-travel—see IDEA 42, *A clean break*.

Try another idea...

"Golf is a good walk spoiled."
MARK TWAIN

Defining idea...

How did it go?

Q **I'm a rabid golf player. Don't tell me I have to give it up and start doing tai chi!**

A *Using huge amounts of water, pesticides, and fertilizers, golf courses often aren't as green as they look. But sustainable golf courses are springing up faster than you can say "Tiger Woods." The pioneer is the Kabi Organic golf course in Queensland, Australia, which is free of any synthetic chemicals. Greens are hand-weeded, the clubhouse menu is organic, and toilets are the composting kind. Another pioneer is Benalup Golf Club in southern Spain, which has introduced a special polymer under the grass to drastically cut down its need for water. Sustainable golfing may take a while to catch on elsewhere, but there is no harm in asking your club if it has plans to go greener, even if it's just ordering in organic coffee!*

Q **What is a green, cheap sport that the whole family can enjoy outdoors in the city?**

A *Try Ultimate Frisbee, a surprisingly addictive and speedy team sport that is played—you guessed it—with a flying disc. It is suitable for all ages and abilities and is one of the fastest-growing sports around, played at both a recreational and competitive level. The only piece of equipment you need is the Frisbee itself, and you can find these made from recycled material such as CD cases and Tetra Pak containers very inexpensively.*

29

Pets count, too

If you want your pet to be green, it certainly doesn't mean buying a frog!

You can reduce your pet's carbon paw-print, and keep them happy and healthy at the same time.

Pets are great, but they are also a long-term commitment, involving demands on both time and money.

The most popular pets are obviously dogs and cats, and many people love the idea of a cute, cuddly kitten or puppy. But before you head for the breeder, think about whether you could offer a home to an unwanted pet. Tens of thousands of dogs and cats are dumped each year, so why not visit an animal rescue center and choose a pet who could do with a home?

Once your furry friend is established, you can buy it toys made from recycled materials or sustainable fibers such as hemp. These days, you can even get pet beds made with organic cotton or recycled PET bottles.

Scrap yarn and fabric can easily be transformed into pet toys with some basic crafty know-how. And they wouldn't have had to be trucked thousands of miles just to get slobbered on.

The bottom line when it comes to reducing your pet's carbon paw-print is dealing with its poop. This is especially true in urban areas where your dog's or cat's pavement decoration gets washed into water courses and ponds, where its bacteria can starve ponds of oxygen and kill aquatic life. Cat feces can harbor nasty parasites such as toxoplasma gondii, which has been known to survive sewage treatment and destroy sea life. If you're a dog owner, you'll already know to bag it and trash it, but you could go a step further and use biodegradable dog poop bags, made from corn starch and vegetable oil, as a greener alternative.

Pets can contribute to noise pollution—dogs in particular. Often this is simply due to boredom. Ensure your dog has a stimulating environment and don't leave it alone for too long.

Then there's the impact pets can have on wildlife. Keep your cat indoors at night when it is likely to hunt. You might also consider putting bells around its collar—the sonic variety are most effective in alerting birds.

Think carefully before you buy an exotic pet such as a tarantula, reptile, or wild bird. They can be tricky to look after and there are increasing numbers of alien species being released into the countryside where they spread disease and damage native wildlife.

FOOD

While dog food (not tested on animals) has a theoretically positive environmental impact as it uses up meat by-products, producing meat is only about a tenth as efficient as growing crops. If you feel strongly about this, there is no reason why your dog can't have a meat-free diet, although cats can't be veggies without supplements.

Defining idea…

"What benefits the animals benefits the people, too."
CÉSAR CHÁVEZ

Natural and organic pet foods use meats that are raised in low-chemical, humane ways without added drugs or hormones. Certified-organic pet food is pricier than the standard variety, but worth it if you consider that it is meeting strict standards that spell out how ingredients are produced and processed.

If you want to take animal rearing a step further, try your hand with chickens, pigs, or bees—see IDEA 30, *The home farm*.

Try another idea…

COMPOST THEIR POOP

Most of our pets' poop either winds up in a landfill, where it's embalmed in plastic bags, or sits on the ground until the next rainstorm washes it into the sewer where it can drift on down to rivers and beaches. You can compost the poop, but not in your usual compost pile, as it doesn't reach high enough temperatures to kill pathogens such as E. coli., which could in turn reach your homegrown produce.

If you have room in your garden, you can bury an old bin a safe distance away from your vegetable garden to use as a pet-waste composter. Or you can buy purpose-made pet waste composters/septic tanks at large department stores or online.

There are green options for cat litter, too. Don't buy the clay kind, as it doesn't rot, meaning it takes up space and is hard to get rid of. So stick to litter made from recycled material such as sawmill scrap or waste from wheat or corn. It's biodegradable, flushable, lighter, and smells less.

When your pet dies, dispose of it thoughtfully. There are green burial and cremation options for pets as well as humans, and don't flush fish down the toilet, even if they're dead, as they can spread disease.

"The greatness of a nation and its moral progress can be judged by the way its animals are treated."

MAHATMA GANDHI

Defining idea…

How did it go?

Q **I hate the idea of all the packaging, transporting, and manufacturing issues around commercial pet food, even if it's organic. Can't I just make my own?**

A *The organic, eco-friendly dog's dinner is already having its day, but you can take things further and make your own as long as you follow a few guidelines. Don't use raw meat, even organic, as it may contain pathogens such as the salmonella bacteria. Anything with small or cooked bones is a no-no because of the risk of splintering, which can lead to internal damage (but a large, raw bone is fine). Bread, too, is off the menu as it could get stuck in your pet's teeth, causing decay. You should always consult your vet before starting a new diet for your pet.*

Q **Are there any environmentally friendly dog and cat cleaners?**

A *If you avoid using chemically-based shampoos for your own hair, if figures that your pets deserve similar treatment, so lather up your cats, dogs, and other furry pets with natural cleaning products. Avoid toxic flea and tick repellents, too, as they can build up and poison wildlife and pets alike. Try natural remedies based on citrus extracts, neem, tea tree, lavender, or linalool; make regular use of a flea comb; and vacuum frequently. Dog food flavored with brewer's yeast and garlic is also a natural flea repellent.*

30

The home farm

Love organic eggs, wild honey, and home-cured ham? Then why not produce your own?

It's something of an urban craze, but keeping a couple of hens or a pig or two could be more than a passing fad.

What could be nicer than eating organic, free-range eggs that were freshly laid just minutes ago in your own backyard? As the eco-movement gathers momentum, there's been a huge surge of interest in growing your own, and that includes pigs, chickens, ducks, and bees.

And this may especially appeal if you hate the idea of intensive farming. Keeping your own puts you in touch with the whole process of rearing, and possibly slaughtering, livestock. Livestock can lend a hoof in the garden, too—pigs will root around, clearing and fertilizing ground ready for planting; chickens will peck away at soil pests and apply a light coating of manure to a cleared vegetable bed. Bees will provide free pollination services and ducks will eat your slugs.

These are probably the most practical choice for the (very) small livestock owner—most people don't own a large enough piece of land for cows or sheep, and goats are a go only if you don't mind them chomping up every single growing thing they

Here's an idea for you... If you're unsure about committing to keeping livestock, why not adopt a battery hen coming to the end of its egg-laying life, but not yet ready for that great big hen coop in the sky? You'll need a patch of ground for them to roam, and a good sturdy shed to lock them in at night—many people simply adapt a standard garden shed with perches and nest boxes. As a guide, a 6' x 4' shed will comfortably accommodate 12–15 hens. You'll also need a little time and patience to oversee their rehabilitation into the real world. Most retired battery hens will live around two to three years, and may produce a small quantity of eggs.

come into contact with. Geese are fine for the country—they produce great eggs and meat—but their noisy hissing may make you unpopular with your neighbors!

Chickens are probably the most straightforward choice as garden livestock. They are unobtrusive, don't smell, and aren't noisy (so long as you don't keep a rooster). You need a good-size garden, but it doesn't have to be huge. Chickens need housing to protect them from foxes, and a grass-based run on which they can be "rotated" so they have access to a fresh, clean patch. Depending on the breed, each hen can produce 100–300 eggs per year, so if you and your family are seriously into eggs you may need a few chickens.

The hens are inexpensive to buy, and their house can be homemade from wood and wire, but needs to be sturdy and secure to protect from foxes and badgers.

DUCKS

Ducks can thrive in gardens, but their own pond is essential. Ducks do have one distinct advantage for any organic gardener: They eat slugs. The cost of duck-keeping is similar to chickens.

BEES

Perhaps surprisingly, bees make very good urban livestock, partly due to the large variety of plants and flowers you find in cities. Honey is full of minerals and natural compounds, and can be eaten on organic bread or cakes, in tea or coffee, or made into mead; the beeswax can be used for candles—a completely eco-friendly lighting source.

More and more of us are turning to our gardens and even window boxes for organic produce—see IDEA 34, *Grow your own*.

Try another idea...

PIGS

At the top end of the urban livestock scale are pigs. Pigs need plenty of space, at least forty-two square yards per pig, preferably more, and as they are intelligent, sociable animals, you need to allow enough room for a few. There are also rules about pig ownership, and your site may need to be assessed first. (An alternative is to "outsource" pig-keeping to someone who will raise the rare-breed pig of your choice and deliver it ready for the freezer.)

Unlike in the olden days, health and safety rules mean you are no longer allowed to feed kitchen scraps to pigs, although homegrown food straight from the vegetable patch is permitted.

Anyone thinking about keeping pigs should be prepared for its eventual slaughter. Squeamish? Well, you can console yourself that the pig has led a happy life and has been humanely killed.

"I like pigs. Dogs look up to us. Cats look down on us. Pigs treat us as equals."
WINSTON CHURCHILL

Defining idea...

How did it go?

Q   How many chickens should I buy?

A   *It depends on how many eggs you want! You and your family may love boiled eggs every day for breakfast, or you may enjoy having spare eggs to give away to friends and family. You can even use them to barter for other things from your neighbors. Good layers will pop one out almost every day, so get as many chickens as you think you need. Six is normally plenty for a family.*

Q   My neighbors are a bit fussy. How do I broach the subject of my livestock to them?

A   *If your neighbors seem disapproving of the new additions to your family, invite them to meet them—chances are they'll be charmed. Offer them a share of the eggs, or the odd jar of honey, and they'll soon come around.*

Q   I'm very sentimental—how will I cope if one of my animals dies?

A   *If you are likely to get very attached then keeping, say, pigs with the intention of slaughtering them eventually may not be for you. It might be less taxing on your emotions to keep chickens and allow them to die of natural causes rather than roasting—or bees, as it's pretty hard to get attached to insects! If one of your livestock does die, you can ask a vet to come and collect the body and dispose of it for you.*

31

Garden green

Once you've made up your mind to garden organically, there's no turning back!

Going organic in your garden means you're protecting your very own little piece of the planet.

It doesn't much matter whether you're looking for a flower-filled garden worthy of a horticultural show or a piece of land that's strictly for fruits and vegetables: gardening without the use of pesticides and other chemicals brings its own challenges and rewards.

Organic gardening aims to be sustainable, ensuring the land and its resources will be available for future generations. This means reducing pollution of the environment and not using pesticides that may be harmful to health and wildlife.

Many gardeners swear that their organic crops are tastier than those grown with artificial chemicals, and most agree that once you've got the hang of it, organic gardening is no harder than the conventional way. You'll also have the peace of mind of knowing exactly what has gone into your soil as well as the pleasure of seeing what comes out of it.

Your plants will also be better off with organic gardening. Chemicals and poisons might work in the short term but as insects and diseases mutate and become resis-

Here's an idea for you...

Draw up a plan of your organic garden before you get planting, either on paper or using a garden design computer program. Having the design in front of you will help you incorporate plenty of variety, which is the key to the successful organic garden, and plan large features such as ponds or wild areas. Resist the temptation to go for a quick makeover—a piecemeal approach, with haphazard features and unsuitable materials, tends to have patchy results. The idea is to create a mini ecosystem; a balanced, integrated environment that can sustain itself through a large range of different species all playing different but connected roles.

tant to particular sprays, they become increasingly ineffective. Pesticides also kill just as many beneficial insects as pests.

Make sure that you use organic methods for the whole garden, not just selected areas, and use organically grown seeds where available. Get rid of your old pesticides and weed killers—ask your local government how you can safely dispose of them.

GETTING STARTED

Rule number one in organic gardening is to improve your soil. You can dig in or spread around organic matter such as leaf mold, composted bark, and garden compost. You'll soon find their bulk will improve the drainage of heavy soils and allow dry soil to hold on to moisture and nutrients.

You can also add in your own homemade compost. Fill a large compost bin with layers of prunings, peelings, eggshells, tea bags, old flower heads, and even bits of cardboard for a nutrient-rich compost. Mix together a good blend of different materials and textures. If your garden is small, try a compact worm bin.

You don't need a strong weed killer—prevent growth with a carpet of bark mulch, leaf mold, or composted straw across soil. Watch the soil like a hawk—if any weeds do dare to show their faces, pull them up or hoe them before they have a chance to set seed. You can add weed seedlings to your compost bin, but bag up tough weeds separately and wait until they decompose before you compost them.

There could be all kinds of nasty chemicals hiding in your garden shed. Find out how to dispose of them in IDEA 10, *Always read the label.*

Try another idea...

Get to know your soil type and buy plants that suit it and the position you put them in—strong plants are less likely to succumb to diseases or pests. Choose naturally disease-resistant varieties whenever you can.

All gardens have pests, but don't reach for a chemical spray when your plants come under attack; encourage natural predators instead. Hedgehogs and toads will eat up slugs and snails, while lacewings and ladybugs have a voracious appetite for aphids. Install bug boxes and piles of stones or logs for creatures to hibernate in, and have some kind of water feature, even if it's only a tiny pond.

Prevent major problems by regularly checking plants. A few aphids can be hosed off before they become a problem and diseased plant parts can be removed at an early stage.

If you still have a pest problem, you can buy biological controls such as tiny parasitic wasps that can be used to control whitefly in greenhouses and a microscopic worm that kills vine weevil grubs.

"When we heal the earth, we heal ourselves."

DAVID ORR, environmentalist

Defining idea...

If you plan to grow vegetables, place strongly scented plants such as French marigolds alongside crops so they either confuse pests or attract them away. Change the position of your vegetable crops each year to prevent the buildup of diseases in the soil.

How did
it go?

Q   Where should I put an organic vegetable patch?

A   *If you plan to grow organic vegetables and fruit, they will need plenty of sun, so the best plot is in the southeast portion of your garden where they'll benefit from maximum sunshine. Vegetable patches should also be on an area of flat ground, because if it's uneven then pools of water will collect that can rot plant roots. If it's on a steep slope the water will drain off before the roots can absorb any water. Leave room for a path or walkway so you don't tread on the soil each time you tend your veggies.*

Q   My free time is limited—won't being an organic gardener take up even more of it?

A   *Much of organic gardening is about prevention rather than cure, but as long as you are prepared to keep a close eye on your garden to tackle problems before they take hold there's no reason why it should take longer. It can take a few years for an organic garden to settle down and form its own ecosystem. But it's not difficult to change your style of gardening and while it might initially feel daunting, you will certainly reap the benefits long-term.*

32

The low-water garden

Is your garden swallowing up more than its fair share of water?

Use resources carefully and your low-water garden can be as fun and colorful as it is sustainable.

When temperatures soar, our water usage both outside and in rockets, too—the average garden hose delivers 1,000 liters of water an hour!

Fresh water supplies are seriously under threat thanks to increased demand and global warming, and every one of us has to cut back on how much water we use— and that means in the garden, too.

Luckily, water efficient gardens can reduce your water bills and running costs; they require less maintenance and use the available space in the most practical way, allowing you to get the most out of your garden.

As with all things gardening related, the soil is the place to start—a healthy, well-maintained soil with plenty of organic matter will retain moisture and nutrients. If you're choosing new plants, make sure you look for varieties that are drought tolerant, too.

Here's an idea for you... **One of your key tasks as a low-water gardener is to apply mulch early in the growing season before the soil starts to dry out. Mulch is a layer of material placed on the soil's surface that reduces water evaporation, keeps down weeds, and improves the soil's condition. It can be made from natural materials such as chipped bark, cocoa shells, manure, homemade compost, grass cuttings, or straw. You can even plant new shrubs and trees through plastic sheeting. Mulched flower beds need considerably less water than those with bare soils. And the thicker the mulch, the more effective it is—a mulch of at least 2 to 4 inches will make a big difference.**

Low-maintenance alternatives to planted areas include gravel, colored glass nuggets, and decking.

Lawns are the thirstiest part of a garden. Letting the grass grow longer helps shade the soil and reduces the need for water. If you must water your lawn, remember that less frequent soaking is better than regular sprinkling as it encourages the roots to search for water stored deep below the soil's surface.

RAIN AND GRAYWATER

Your best investment at times of drought is a water butt, or two if your garden is big enough—many water firms sell them at a discount. A water butt (or underground tank) collects water runoff from roofs and gutters and provides vital water supplies when things dry up.

Graywater from baths and showers can be used safely on most nonedible plants, provided it is applied to the soil rather than foliage and not left long enough for bacteria to grow.

WATERING

When water is in short supply, don't use watering-can roses (except for seedlings), as the water goes all over the place instead of directly to the roots where it is needed. Use a narrow head instead. Water in the early morning or in the evening to avoid evaporation.

Make sure your garden hose doesn't have any wasteful leaks, and fit it with a trigger to control the flow. An aerating nozzle allows you to water roots without washing away the soil or having to use the less efficient spray pattern. If your garden is important to you, look into low-water irrigation systems.

Other water saving measures

- Plant new shrubs, vegetables, or plants in a saucer-shaped dip of soil so the water pools around them.
- Cut off the mouths of plastic bottles and bury them upside down next to new plants. Water into these and they'll channel the water straight to the roots.
- Feed lawns and other plants with fertilizer to help them grow new roots and make the best use of the water in the soil.
- Invest time in eliminating water-stealing weeds as soon as they show themselves in spring.
- Buy and plant new plants as early in the season as possible so they can grow roots before dry weather begins. Reduce watering once the roots are established.
- Limit hanging baskets and small containers unless you can keep them in shady spots. Larger containers are easier to keep watered and proportionally use less water.

Try another idea...

For more hints on how to save water around the home, see **IDEA 17, If in drought...**

Defining idea...

"A garden is half made when it is well planned."
LIBERTY HYDE BAILEY, horticulturist

Q   **What kind of plants thrive in a dry garden?**

A   *The secret of "dry" gardening is to use plants that thrive on little water
naturally. Gray- or silver-leaved, fleshy, and small-leaved plants do well.
Think Mediterranean: Heat-loving plants such as lavender, rock rose, and
some euphorbia can chug along quite happily without extra watering. Sage,
thyme, and rosemary all like warm, dry conditions and produce aromatic
foliage—great for summer barbecues. Choose bedding plants that aren't too
thirsty—pelargoniums, begonias, nasturtiums, and petunias should all thrive.*

Q   **How do I know when my garden really needs watering?**

A   *Aside from obvious signs such as wilting, before you even consider watering push aside the mulch, stick your fingers or a spade into the soil, and if
it is moist below the surface you don't need to water. It's all too easy to
over-water plants, and some, like lavender, can be watered to death! One
good soak every ten days is better than a daily sprinkle.*

Q   **When is the best time to start making my garden more water
efficient?**

A   *High summer is not the best time to plan a water-wise garden. Carry out
your usual maintenance, but don't put in young plants, start a new grass
lawn, or install a new irrigation system. The ground is hard, disturbed soil
will lose a lot more water, and new plants are far more likely to die. Wait
for autumn, when temperatures drop and some rain arrives. It will be easier
and more successful, and plants will have plenty of time to get established.*

33

Lovely, leafy compost

A homemade garden compost improves the soil, recycles organic matter, and helps conserve water. What's more, it's absolutely free!

Are you hot to rot? Then get composting!

I could never quite figure out how a horrible slimy mix of old fruit peels, eggshells, paper, tea bags, and grass cuttings could eventually turn into a rich, brown compost that almost looked good enough to eat. But nature's a wonderful thing, and now that I'm an avid compost maker I've seen the transformation myself.

The rules of compost making are pretty easy. At its most basic level you can simply throw everything in a huge pile and wait for it to rot down, but there are other ways that provide faster and better mixes that will do wonders for your garden.

WHAT CAN I COMPOST?

If it can rot, it can compost, but some things, like grass cuttings and soft young weeds, break down quickly. They work as "hotter rotters," or activators, getting the composting started, but on their own will decay to little more than a mushy mess.

Older and tougher plant material is slower to rot but gives body to the finished compost. Woody items decay very slowly, so they are best chopped or shredded first.

Here's an idea for you...

In a hurry? Then learn how to speed up your compost. It can take up to a year for your organic waste to break down, but there are ways of helping things along. Cutting the ingredients up into small pieces introduces oxygen into the compost; this helps the organic matter to decompose faster. A compost shredder is useful to chop up larger and coarser material. Mixing and turning the compost also helps it decompose faster. Positioning your composter where it gets some sunshine can help, too, but if it's in full sun this may dry out the compost too much.

Compost ingredients

Hotter rotters (activators):

- Comfrey leaves
- Young weeds
- Grass cuttings
- Chicken manure

Other compostable items:

- Wood ash
- Cardboard
- Paper towels/bags
- Eggshells
- Fruit and vegetable scraps
- Tea bags
- Coffee grounds
- Old flowers and plants
- Old straw/hay
- Strawy manures
- Soft prunings
- Perennial weeds
- Gerbil, hamster, and rabbit bedding

Defining idea...

"Man has only a thin layer of soil between himself and starvation."

BARD OF CINCINNATI

Slow rotters:

- Autumn leaves
- Tough hedge clippings
- Woody prunings

146

- Sawdust
- Wood shavings

Best avoided:

- Meat
- Fish
- Newspaper
- Cooked food

Banned!

- Coal/coke ash
- Cat litter
- Dog waste
- Disposable diapers
- Glossy magazines

Once your compost is "cooked" why not use it to help along your own produce as outlined in IDEA 34, *Grow your own*.

Try another idea…

"We might say that the earth has the spirit of growth; that its flesh is the soil."
LEONARDO DA VINCI

Defining idea…

MAKING COMPOST

A good compost heap is like a good cake: light, moist, and made up of layers! And like a cake, texture is key.

When you start your compost bin or heap, choose a sunny spot in the garden on well-drained, level ground. Fork the soil over lightly, then put a layer of scrunched up or shredded paper on the ground. There are two types of material: "green" (grass clippings, fruit and vegetable waste, soft weeds, etc.); and "brown" (e.g., cardboard, straw, woody trimmings, old leaves), which need to be added in roughly equal amounts. Add them chopped up, in light layers if possible.

If the material is very dense and compacted or very finely shredded, add some more scrunched up paper or ripped up cardboard to keep air pockets in the mix.

You can also add a few handfuls of soil, some well-rotted compost from another heap, or some horse manure. This will encourage the helpful microorganisms to colonize your new heap quickly.

To keep the heap moist and warm, cover it with an old piece of carpet or put a lid on it.

A good heap will start to heat up as the rotting process takes place. The hotter it is, the faster it rots and some heaps will reach 140 degrees F if they are big enough and have the right materials in them.

If you want to get compost going faster you will need at least ten cubic feet of material that must be turned over frequently in a wooden container or open heap; a lot of work but you'll get the finished compost in around two months.

ADDITIVES TO MAKE BETTER COMPOST

You can add special compost activators to speed up the compost process, usually mixtures of naturally occurring microorganisms.

You can also add your own: An occasional handful of soil, ready compost from another heap, or even horse manure will supply your heap with beneficial microorganisms.

You can also introduce composting worms ("brandling" or "tiger worms," not common earthworms) which can be bought at garden centers or over the Internet.

Q **I have lots of perennial weeds in my garden. Can I add them to my compost heap?**

A *Some perennial weeds will be killed in a compost heap so long as its internal temperature is high enough. Avoid really persistent stranglers such as ground elder and bindweed, but don't burn or dump them, since they are rich in plant foods. Mix them with grass mowings in a plastic sack. Tie it up and leave for a few months until the weeds deteriorate into mush, then add the mix to the compost heap.*

Q **Will my compost heap attract pests?**

A *Compost is made by a host of small and microscopic creatures that help break matter down to create the end result. These are not pests and will not overrun your garden. Rats may visit a compost heap if they are already in the area, so if you are worried use a container with a lid and keep it closed.*

Q **I've tried making compost before and it's just ended up as a slimy, smelly mess—any tips?**

A *The secret to good compost is incorporating a mix of different materials and textures. If, for instance, you only use grass cuttings, you will end up with nutrient-poor sludge that is OK to spread around as a mulch but not much else. Use a broad range of ingredients for a rich, beneficial compost.*

How did it go?

34

Grow your own

Whether you own a window box or a meadow, every outdoor space can yield a fine crop of organic fruits and veggies.

Join the growing number of gardeners who are setting aside a little patch for organically grown crops of all varieties.

What could be nicer than preparing a meal from produce grown in your very own garden? Growing vegetables and fruits successfully is no different from growing any other plant. Start with good plants or seeds, give them what they want—food, water, and light—and they'll do the work for you.

You don't need a huge plot to grow your own. Plant some delicious cut-and-come-again salads in a window box, plan a "square foot" garden on a four-foot square plot, or use your flower bed to grow decorative vegetables and flowers together.

If you garden organically you'll avoid using sprays that could harm children, pets, and wildlife. You'll be working with nature, rather than against it, managing pests and diseases with care and vigilance. You'll make compost from garden and kitchen waste, so as well as reducing the amount that goes to landfill sites you'll be producing a useful organic soil improver, which will make your garden more fertile without costing you a penny.

If you've only got room for one crop this year, make it zucchini. Well known for its prolific cropping, this surefire summer squash is easy to cultivate from either seed or plant, and can even be grown in a pot. Cooked as a vegetable (though technically a fruit), organically grown zucchinis have a light, sweet, slightly nutty flavor. They are a good source of vitamins A and C, potassium, antioxidants, and fiber. You can use the colorful flowers in a variety of recipes: stuffed, sautéed, baked, and in soup. The tubular green zucchini is the most familiar, but colors range from black through various shades of gray, green, yellow, and even white, and some varieties are round or bottle-shaped.

Growing your own food doesn't have to be time-consuming or expensive. A few packages of seeds and some basic tools—a spade, fork, hoe, rake, trowel, and watering can—will provide you with all you need to fill a plot with vegetables. Look out for good quality second-hand tools if money's tight.

Growing your own can be addictive, so if you need more space at a later stage, you could look into getting a plot in a community garden.

Don't forget that, as well as being fun, growing your own food is a healthy, productive, and sustainable activity. You can involve the whole family: children will benefit enormously from learning where food comes from, and they may like to have their own little patch. Why not get a group of friends together to run one or several plots, approach your local school, health authority, or housing association and ask them to help you develop a food growing project?

SETTING UP YOUR PLOT

When you're thinking about where to grow fruit and vegetables in your garden, try to find a sunny spot with good drainage. A south-facing aspect is ideal, with no overhanging tree branches and shade cast by buildings or hedges. Avoid the area next to hedges as this tends to be dry. Provide shelter from wind, and protection, such as netting or chicken wire, from wildlife, such as birds or squirrels.

Fruit and vegetable plots require quite a lot of work—planting, weeding, watering, tying, harvesting, manuring, and so on. So make your life as easy as possible by designing the plot ergonomically—making it low maintenance.

Divide the plot into four areas—this enables you to rotate the crops, minimizing disease problems.

SAVING SPACE

There's room for a few organic fruits and vegetables in any garden, no matter how small. You can grow vegetables among ornamentals (or vice versa), or make the most of vertical spaces, such as with a runner bean "hedge," or grow beans, gourds, cucumbers, or melons over a willow teepee frame.

Lots of varieties are happy in pots or growing bags if you look after them well. Buy ready-grown plants of sweet pepper, zucchinis, climbing beans, chili pepper, cherry tomato, eggplant, and strawberries, or try herbs or salad leaves grown from seed.

For larger fruit bushes such as blueberries, figs, peaches, and apricots, select a larger pot and make sure you check the compost requirements on the plant label.

And now you're all set up to use your own organic produce in jams, chutneys, and pickles. See how in IDEA 24, *Homemade goodies*.

Try another idea...

"The fruit derived from labor is the sweetest of pleasures."
LUC DE VAUVENARGUES

Defining idea...

153

Q   How do I decide which vegetables to grow?

A   *Grow the ones you like to eat! Try to find disease-resistant varieties that you can harvest progressively to ensure a ready supply of yummy vegetables throughout the growing season. Be prepared to practice crop rotation, too. This involves dividing your plot into four pieces or more, each one home to a different vegetable group that stays together each year but moves onto the next part of the rotation every spring. The vegetables are grouped by family as well as similar feeding habits. All successful organic growers practice crop rotation, as it's the best route to soil fertility and the control of pests and diseases.*

Q   Can I plant crops among my flower borders?

A   *You certainly can. Beneficial insects and wildlife are your best friends when it comes to controlling pests in your garden and vegetable patch. Planting simple annuals among your vegetables, such as Californian poppies and marigolds, will attract a host of beneficial insects like ladybugs and hoverflies who will munch up your aphids. There are other ways to encourage wildlife in your garden to eat pests and their eggs: Plant a few native shrubs and herbaceous perennials in your garden; create a pond; leave a small pile of logs in the corner of your yard; and feed the birds throughout the winter.*

35

The good–and green– companions

Think you're something of a matchmaker? Pairing up works for plants as well as people, so get plotting.

Companion planting is the canny route to totally organic gardening and a way to understand just how smart nature can be.

It worked for Greek and Roman gardeners, and thousands of years on it still works for their modern-day counterparts—companion planting is one of the simplest ways you can go organic. By grouping certain plants together you can use their natural properties to boost pest control and improve growth. Companion planting also fosters a deeper understanding of what it means to be an organic gardener.

For instance, a particular plant may add nutrients to the soil, or it may distract pests or lure beneficial insects. Others may protect delicate plants from the sun and wind. As gardeners, we can build thriving plant communities by giving each plant the right type of soil, shelter, aspect, and treatment.

Here's an idea for you...

If you're new to companion planting, you can't get a better friend than nasturtiums. These sunny, golden-orange flowers—a favorite of the painter Monet—can reduce your need for insecticides. When grown with ornamentals and vegetables, nasturtium makes a good aphid control in the garden since they attract them away from other plants. The flowers also attract hoverflies that feed on aphids. These flexible friends have another use: They make a good crop in themselves as their flowers, leaves, and pickled seeds can all be added into a mixed salad to give color, flavor, and texture.

Many plants attract bees and butterflies. By supporting insect populations plants increase the number of hardworking pollinators, predators, and parasites, which are a natural part of a healthy garden. Plants may also attract birds and other creatures that prey on pests and are generally beneficial.

Many pests locate their food by smell, so combining strong-smelling plants such as marigolds with susceptible crops will cause confusion and reduce attacks. Other strongly scented deterrents include rosemary, thyme, sage, lavender, chives, wormwood, and garlic.

Marigolds are also loved by hoverflies, which help keep down aphids. Other flowers that are rich in nectar and attract pest predators include echinacea, coreopsis, and aster. Wild flowers also attract beneficial bugs so if you have the space, section off a corner of your garden.

Learn more about organic gardening in IDEA 31, *Garden green*.

Try another idea…

PLANTING COMBINATIONS THAT WORK

- Asparagus contain a substance called asparagin that repels tomato pests.
- Borage attracts bees, accumulates minerals for the compost heap, and grows well with strawberries.
- Carrots and leeks or onions can be planted together to protect against a number of pests: leeks repel carrot fly and carrots repel onion fly and leek moth.
- Chamomile is known as the physician plant because it perks up anything planted in or around it.
- Chives have an onion-like scent that wards off aphids from chrysanthemums, sunflowers, carrots, fruits, and tomatoes.
- Cucumbers do well with cabbages nearby. By the time you plant cucumber seeds the cabbages should be thriving, so when the temperature rises the cucumber vines can shelter from the hot sun under the cabbage leaves.
- Foxgloves accumulate minerals in their leaves and are beneficial to all parts of the garden, stimulating the growth of plants.
- Garlic deters aphids and is particularly good planted with roses and raspberries.
- Lemon balm attracts bees for pollination.
- Nasturtiums are another great flower in the garden as they keep aphids, cabbage worms, Colorado beetles, squash bugs, and whitefly at bay.

"Gardens are not made by singing 'Oh, how beautiful,' and sitting in the shade."
RUDYARD KIPLING

Defining idea…

157

- Peas, beans, sweet peas, and lupins have an ability to fix nitrogen—they convert it by way of bacteria that live in the roots into a form that can be used easily by plants. Peas are happy with lettuce, beans, carrots, radish, cucumbers, corn, and turnips.
- Radishes and cucumbers do better planted close to each other. As the radishes are harvested the cucumbers can fill out the center area. Radishes can also be planted in the same row as carrots because the radishes will germinate rapidly and loosen the soil for the later emerging carrots. The carrots are left to fill in the spaces left by the harvested radishes.
- Tagetes (African and French marigold) deters aphids and whitefly through scent and by attracting hoverflies. Marigold roots secrete chemicals that help stop bindweed.
- Yarrow boosts vigor in other plants and accumulates phosphorous, calcium, and silica, which can benefit homemade compost. It attracts many beneficial creatures such as hoverflies and ladybugs.

Q   How can I plan my garden with companion planting in mind?

A   Think about the structure of your garden. Hedges can curb the worst extremes of the weather and reduce wind speed and, lower down, leafy ground cover under plants such as clematis keeps roots cool and moist, which are ideal growing conditions. Cool weather crops (e.g., spinach and lettuce) thrive between hotter weather crops (tomatoes). The tomatoes will shield the spinach and lettuce from the hot sun but allow enough sunlight through. Birds can be encouraged with plants offering perches, shelter, and food from fruits and berries. Dense plantings shelter and attract hedgehogs, frogs, and toads who eat pests.

Q   Will companion planting really help reduce the amount of pesticide I use?

A   Increasingly scientific evidence shows that certain plant combinations really do keep down the pest population naturally. For example a trial carried out under controlled conditions found that when carrots were planted with onions, carrot fly damage was reduced by 20 percent without affecting the yield, and growing carrots with leeks greatly reduced the levels of pest damage to the leeks. Growing nasturtiums with cabbages increased the numbers of beneficial insects. Nine out of ten trialists who grew a tomato/ French marigold combination felt that they had fewer problems with whitefly compared to previous years, and 86 percent said the spider mite populations were greatly reduced by the planting. What more could you wish for?

36

Your very own mini eco-park

Turn your backyard into a natural haven for useful insects, birds, frogs, and other welcome visitors.

No garden? No problem! Even the tiniest window box can host its own mini ecosystem.

Biodiversity may be under threat from urbanization, but we can all do our part for wildlife by creating small-scale nature reserves in backyards, gardens, and balconies. Encouraging a wide range of different species is one of the most planet friendly steps you can take, as it helps preserve the delicate balance of the local ecosystem, without which we simply could not survive.

While the individual garden may be modest, it can still be a rich haven for wildlife, and a whole load of gardens together in a neighborhood can combine to form a veritable Serengeti!

And you can make all the difference by ensuring you have the right conditions for wildlife to thrive in your garden. The key to encouraging birds and beasts is variety, whether of structure, design, or planting. So, experiment with lots of different shapes and species by all means, but bear in mind that your garden should work as a cohesive whole, with features linked together so that wildlife can move between them easily rather than having a series of isolated features.

Here's an idea for you...

Even the tiniest water feature will help make your garden a haven for wildlife. A pond is ideal, but a bowl or half barrel will do, encouraging frogs, hedgehogs, and other wildlife that will feed on bugs and snails. Dragonflies will often breed in ponds, and birds will visit to drink and bathe. If you have room for a pond, site it in a sunny position away from overhanging trees and ensure the sides are slightly sloping, so birds can access it, amphibians can spawn, and hedgehogs can escape if they fall in. Top it up with rainwater from a butt, as this is better for plants and saves water in times of drought.

Having several different heights is important, both with physical structures (fences, sheds, etc.) and planting. It will help maximize space, too. Use vertical surfaces such as trellises to grow climbing plants either in the soil or in containers that will add interest and provide valuable homes for wildlife.

Replace worn-out fences with wildlife-supporting hedging, plant at least one tree for birds and insects to enjoy, and plan a range of contours: emphasize an existing slope, create a bank, or shape borders into gentle curves.

Try leaving part of your lawn uncut to create a habitat for grasshoppers, beetles, and young amphibians, and provide roosts for insects such as damselflies. Include some wildflowers to add interest and more wildlife value.

When it comes to the flower borders, variety is again the key. Sunny, sheltered, nectar-rich borders will attract bees and butterflies. Choose plants that flower at different times throughout the year so there is a steady supply of nectar throughout the season.

Don't be too obsessive about clearing out cracks and gaps in paving slabs—they provide

Defining idea...

"You could say that gardens are our biggest nature reserve."

BILL ODDIE, broadcaster and ornithologist

another valuable habitat for wildlife and many low-growing plants will happily live in the gaps.

Find out more about ways of natural gardening in IDEA 31, Garden green.

Try another idea...

One of the best ways of encouraging wildlife into a garden is to build a water feature, anything from an old bucket to a designer wildlife pond.

If one area of your garden is boggy, make the most of it by planting moisture-loving plants and create another habitat. If you are planning a pond, include a marshy area nearby.

Recycle your organic kitchen and garden waste to create a compost heap that will provide you with a wonderful soil conditioner and at the same time host invertebrates and other animals—a rich feeding ground for birds and beetles.

Dead wood can be used to create a simple wood pile or interesting sculptural feature, and is a useful habitat for lots of different invertebrates. A pile of stones does a similar job, too.

You can easily help wildlife with features such as bird and bat boxes, solitary bee nests, and bird feeders. Birds can be provided with food, either bought seed or food scraps, throughout the year.

Think carefully about the origin of anything you buy for your garden. Ensure that plants come from cultivated, not wild, stock and that the use of any material, such as potting compost, does not put a habitat under threat.

"Wildlife doesn't just need the wild—it can thrive in our gardens, too."
DAVID BELLAMY, botanist and broadcaster

Defining idea...

How did
it go?

Q   I don't have much time for gardening. Are there any shortcuts to a wildlife friendly garden?

A   *The simplest way to encourage wildlife is to create a wild corner, which can be a great habitat for birds and insects and a haven for larger mammals. The ideal place is behind a shed or in a rarely visited corner of the garden. Thick hedges are good for nesting birds, and thistles, grasses, nettles, and some wildflowers attract moths, hoverflies, and butterflies. Encouraging flying insects to your garden may in turn attract bats and birds that hunt them. A wild corner that becomes damp is useful, as dampness encourages fungi, which recycle the nutrients from plant matter, which in turn helps other plants to grow.*

Q   I live in an apartment. Is there anything I can do to encourage wildlife?

A   *Even a window box can be a mini eco-park! Plant one and you'll get a close-up view of the many small creatures that visit, for instance, ladybugs, and other insects that come to hibernate. Lots of plants, bulbs, and even small shrubs will grow happily in a window box as long as you look after them. Go for native plants, as these attract the most species. Include some plants that flower early and late, so that insects will visit in spring and autumn as well as summer. Feel free to experiment: Try an herb garden, a meadow patch, or use low-growing woodland plants if you have a shady spot.*

37

Right from the start

You love your kids, right? So show it in the way you all live, from diapers onward.

Kids learn from their parents, so teach them about our fragile planet right from the beginning.

If you start your kids off with a green and healthy lifestyle, chances are they'll carry on where you leave off, taking good habits into their own adulthood.

Luckily the choices you make for your children in terms of sustainability are often also healthier and more fun. The downside is that organic food and cotton, certified wooden furniture, and ecotourism can be pricier than their standard equivalents. Still, as parents you can't put a price on your kids, just as you can't put a price on the planet's well-being.

But going green is not only about buying the "right" products for your kids—it's also about what you don't buy. The alarming battery of equipment forced onto new moms is only the start, to be followed by mountains of plastic toys and later by handheld gadgets that eat up electricity and keep the kids indoors.

So, buy the minimum and maintain some healthy cynicism. Take eco baby products, which have become a massive industry. Try to verify any claims being made,

Here's an idea for you... **Save cash and reduce your home's plastic pileup by joining a toy library. The advantages are plentiful, and they are usually very affordable, too. Toy libraries provide good quality educational and play items on loan, mainly for preschool children, and have a range of items covering all aspects of growth and development. You also have access to books, DVDs, CDs, and even video games. Libraries are a hub of activity, and you can meet other parents and carers, share information, and join in activities. And the great thing is that once your child is tired of a certain toy, back it goes for someone else to enjoy, freeing up space for the next big hit!**

and look out for certification from recognized bodies such as the Forest Stewardship Council and the Soil Association.

There are other ways than shopping yourself green: Get your children in touch with their planet, perhaps give them their own patch of garden to look after, let them help you gather or prepare food so they become aware of its origins. As part of the daily routine, teach them to turn off lights and appliances when not in use, recycle leftovers, pick up litter, and walk or cycle rather than drive.

Another way is to cut down on chemicals in your home. Research shows that small children are more vulnerable to the harmful effects of toxins, so reduce cleaning products, antibacterials, PVC products, and fire-retardant furnishings, all of which can contain potentially harmful chemicals.

FEEDING

Obviously breast-feeding is the most sustainable and ecologically sound way to feed a baby, not to mention the cheapest. And, according to a recent report, 95 percent of baby bottles are made from polycarbonate plastic containing bisphenol, a suspected hormone disrupter. So, if you do bottle-feed, go for a reinforced glass bottle or polypropylene.

When your baby gets older, you can shop for organic baby food, or better still, make your own from fresh organic ingredients. That way you can prioritize locally produced, pesticide-free food and get your child into good eating habits right from the start.

Our homes contain many harmful chemicals; find out how to cut back in IDEA 10, *Always read the label.*

Try another idea…

FURNITURE, TOYS, AND EQUIPMENT

Start with the very basics in your nursery, using untreated eco-textiles for curtains and blinds. Tuck your baby up with organic cotton bedding, and decorate with a nontoxic eco-paint. Nylon and other petroleum-based carpets are thought to emit gases that may be carcinogenic, so instead pick a toddler-friendly natural fiber such as soft sisal.

Make sure any wooden nursery furniture you buy new has the FSC logo to show it comes from sustainable sources. Invest in multifunction furniture that has a long life—cots that convert into sofas or high chairs that turn into tables. You can also find recyclable cardboard cots. Better still, think secondhand—ask other parents, or search local neighborhood shops and sales, eBay, or Freecycle.com, an international movement of local recycling networks.

CLOTHES

Conventional cotton production swallows up a quarter of the world's pesticides, so if you can afford it buy organic cotton clothing. Better still, if you borrow clothes or buy

"Wrinkles are hereditary. Parents get them from their children."

DORIS DAY

Defining idea…

secondhand, you are not producing a consumer drive. Scour nearly-new sales, websites, and secondhand shops.

SAVINGS

Some banks offer "green" savings accounts, donating a sum each year to environmental or other good causes. But your kids' savings may not be doing as much for the planet as you'd like. Shop around and make sure you know exactly how much money is likely to be given out. You may find it's more worthwhile to open an account with whoever offers the best interest rate, and then donate the difference in interest saved to an ethical charity.

TEENAGERS

Keep an eye on older children, too, as they may not be as eco-savvy as you'd like them to be. For instance, recent research found that British teenagers' gadgets waste over £100 million ($200 million) worth of electricity every year in standby mode alone. This could be reduced by a third if teens were to switch appliances off rather than leaving them on standby. So get them into good habits as soon as they have their first gadget.

Defining idea…

"Children really brighten up a household. They never turn the lights off."

RALPH BUS

Q   **I'm confused about the diaper debate—reusable or disposable?**

How did it go?

A   *The main problem with disposable diapers is where they end up: in a land-fill, where they may take up to 500 years to decompose! One report sug-gested that by using twenty-four washable diapers and laundering them in an energy-efficient washing machine, parents can reduce global warming and save money even taking into account laundry costs. Your city or town may be able to give you more information, organizing "diaperchinos" that combine a morning coffee with talks on reusable diapers and laundering services, or with subsidized packs or trial kits to help you on your way. Another alternative is compostable diapers, perhaps made from woven bamboo. Experiment to see which diaper suits your child; some suppliers offer a starter pack with a variety of reusable diapers.*

Q   **How can I have a home eco-party for my children?**

A   *Kids' parties have become ever more sophisticated—and wasteful—and often small children don't need or appreciate them. Keep it simple. Fancy extras such as party poppers, streamers, balloons, hats, decorations, and costumes should be kept to a minimum, and where possible homemade and saved to be reused next time. Prepare simple organic food and create your own party bags and invites from recycled paper (the kids will enjoy doing this). Don't use disposable plates and cups—keep tableware for next time. Use natural latex balloons and avoid helium ones—they don't biodegrade and can damage wildlife if allowed to drift away.*

169

38

Lighten up

Maximize the use of natural light in your home, and make the artificial kind energy wise.

Let there be light, by all means. Only not too much of it!

When was the last time you looked up in wonder at a dark, star-filled sky? If it was recently then you are lucky indeed—for most of us it's a rare event, thanks to the steady march of urbanization and its accompanying orange glow.

So the stars are being blotted out by man-made light, but there are other effects, too. Too much unnecessary artificial light is bad for the environment, wasting valuable energy and threatening wildlife. So it makes sense to limit the amount we use but without reducing visual quality.

One way is to use more low-energy compact fluorescent lamps (CFLs) in the home. No longer associated with drab factory settings, today's CFLs are high-quality lamps with good visual properties. An old-fashioned (incandescent) bulb converts only 5 percent of the energy into light. A CFL converts around 25 percent of the energy into light.

Most common bulb types can be found by checking around but for more unusual designs or larger quantities there are a number of suppliers on the Internet.

Here's an idea for you... **Natural daylight is completely free and imparts warmth and energy into any room. Make the most of it, especially during winter months, by keeping your windows as clear as possible. Thick curtains are great for keeping out drafts, but when they are open the heavy, bunched-up fabric can sit across each edge of the window, blocking out those valuable rays. Fit extra-wide rails with some surplus at each end rather than flush with each window edge, so that the curtains can be pulled right to the sides, leaving the glass clear.**

The next generation of lighting is based on LEDs—brighter, white versions of those red and green indicator lamps on most pieces of electronics. These are around 70 percent efficient, nearly seventy times better than the bulbs we use at the moment. And they will probably get better.

Apart from the energy saving aspect, there are other reasons to cut back on lighting. Over-bright or poorly directed lights shining onto neighboring property can affect your neighbors' right to enjoy their own property (for instance, a bright security light shining into a bedroom window).

It can detract from the architectural appearance of a building and even obscure complex or attractive features.

Many birds and animals are affected by stray light intruding into their night world, confusing their natural patterns, deterring them from established foraging areas, and affecting their breeding cycles. This happens in rural areas as well as the city.

Trees provide entire ecosystems to many animal and insect species, and are detrimentally affected by light pollution. Trees need to adjust to seasonal variations, and artificial light prevents them from doing so—many trees are prevented from losing their leaves by bad lighting. This has an effect on the wildlife, such as birds that depend on the trees as their natural habitat.

There are many other ways to save energy. All is revealed in IDEA 13, *Warm and cozy.* *Try another idea...*

Before you install lighting, it's worth asking yourself a few simple questions:

- Is lighting necessary?
- Are the lights angled correctly?
- Could safety or security be achieved by other measures, such as segregation or screening of an area?
- Do the lights have to be on all night?

If lighting is the best option then only the right amount of light for the task should be installed. Lighting will then only become a problem if it is poorly designed or incorrectly installed.

- For domestic security lights a 150-watt lamp is adequate. High-power (300/500W) lamps create too much glare, actually reducing security. All-night porch lights should be low energy.
- Make sure that lights are adjusted to illuminate the area intended and not neighboring property.
- Security lights should be adjusted so that they only pick up the movement of persons in the immediate area and not beyond.
- To reduce the effects of glare, main beam angles of all lights should be below 70 degrees.
- If uplighting has to be used then install shields above the lamp to reduce the amount of wasted upward light.
- Use solar lighting outside where possible.

"Night is a world lit by itself."
ANTONIO PORCHIA, poet

Defining idea...

173

How did it go?

Q   How can I maximize the natural light in my home?

A   *The first thing you can do is let light come through windows without inter-ruptions. Remove objects from windowsills and in the summer replace heavy curtains with lightweight blinds or muslin. Place a large mirror oppo-site the window to reflect light around the room. Choose light and bright paint colors to reflect light. Choose a pale flooring for the same reason—glossy surfaces such as polished wood reflect more light than soft, absor-bent ones like carpet. Keep large, busy patterns to a minimum, especially in small, dark rooms.*

Q   Aren't energy-efficient lightbulbs a little dark?

A   *A Bostonian friend once told me this joke: "How many New Englanders does it take to change a lightbulb? Answer: three. One to change the bulb and two to say how much better the old one was." Well, it's a bit of an exaggeration, but one that hints at our resistance to the new breed of energy saving lightbulbs, or compact fluorescent lamps (CFLs). Detractors say that CFLs start very slowly, don't give the light they promise, or don't last as long as they claim. But quality and performance have improved recently so long as you buy well-known brands and a strong enough watt-age. CFLs will last between six and fifteen years depending on wattage and product type and you'll save a minimum of 75 percent of the energy of an old-fashioned bulb, surely a win–win for the environment and for your energy costs.*

39

Help your PC live a little longer

Your home computer may be the hub of the house but just how green is it?

In the rush to upgrade all things electronic, it's easy to forget how resource-hungry computers can be.

Sometimes I think my PC is my best friend. I use it to work, socialize, play, learn, entertain, calculate, keep in touch, and more. Most American households now have at least one, but just how sustainable is this valuable piece of hardware?

There are lots of environmental issues around information and communications technology (ICT), and that includes other hardware, such as cell phones, printers, modems, accessories, and handheld gadgets: the way equipment is manufactured; how it can be repaired, recycled, or disposed of; the amount of power it uses; and the resource-hungry cycle of updating equipment.

Research by the United Nations University into the environmental impact of personal computers found that around 1.8 tons of raw material are needed to manufacture the average desktop PC and monitor.

If you upgrade a piece of technology, pass on your old one. Your out-of-date PC could be a lifeline for schools and community organizations in the developing world. Dedicated charities will take your old hardware, recondition it, and send it on to people in need. They can also make use of mice, keyboards, modems, cables and power leads, memory, and other peripheral parts. Other items in demand are CD or DVD players/writers, multimedia peripherals, USB devices/cables, multimedia cards (video capture, etc.), modems, and sound cards. Some organizations have a minimum number or specification, while others may like a donation. Get details from your community or the manufacturer.

The UN report concluded that the best way to minimize impact on the environment from a personal computer is to extend its useful life, for instance, by turning off equipment when it is not being used and cutting down on printing. You could also upgrade the memory or hard disk space as much as possible, and use accessories such as a USB wireless stick—a small plug-in that can provide fast wi-fi access. Strip your software down to the essentials—don't use valuable space or processor memory on programs and files you don't use. Keep your computer well-tuned so that it runs more efficiently.

TIME TO SAY GOODBYE

Equipment that is beyond its useful life for you may be of use to someone else, and can be refurbished and passed on to schools, other charities, or individuals.

If hardware fails completely, it must be disposed of carefully, as most of it contains harmful or toxic elements and should not be thrown in the trash.

Many large manufacturers are taking back PCs at the end of their life and using the collected waste in an eco-friendly manner, either by ecological disposal, reuse, or refurbishment. Otherwise ask your local government about the best way to dispose of it.

You can recycle virtually anything. See how in IDEA 4, *Once more with feeling.*

Try another idea…

BUYING GREEN COMPUTERS

If you're buying new, there is no reason why you can't get your hands on a relatively ethical piece of hardware. You'll need to take into account the environmental impact of the manufacturing process, any specific energy-saving features, and how easily the computer can be recycled when you're done with it.

Some companies are producing "carbon neutral" PCs, eliminating toxins from their computers such as polyvinyl chloride (PVC) and brominated flame retardants (BFRs), using recycled components and carbon offsetting, planting trees to offset the power used to run the computers, and offering to recycle any unwanted hardware.

There are several standards that gauge how much energy a PC uses or how it might affect the environment at the end of its life. One standard is the Energy Star label, which takes into account reduced energy consumption, limited use of toxins, ease of recycling, easy upgrades to extend useful life and reduced waste through take-back policy.

For much more detailed information, Epeat (www.epeat.net) is a site that lists a range of manufacturers and compares their products, awarding bronze, silver, and gold status according to various green criteria.

"Why not put a tree in the ground, and not your mobile [phone]?"
SUE HOLDEN, The Woodland Trust

Defining idea…

How did
it go?

Q   Are there such thing as "green" ISPs?

A   *There are a number of possible Internet service providers (ISP) that can help charities raise funds, help with carbon offsetting and manage initiatives such as tree planting. Others are run as not-for-profit workers' collectives or consumer cooperatives, run on ethical, environmentally responsible principles. Look at Friends of the Earth's website (www.foe.org) for more information.*

Q   How can I assess PC makers' "green" credentials?

A   *One way is to check out the Greenpeace website (www.greenpeace.org), where the Green Electronics Guide ranks leading PC and mobile manufacturers on their global policies regarding both their use of toxic chemicals and the degree to which they take responsibility for dealing with the electronic waste (e-waste) generated by their products. The good thing is that it's updated quarterly, so information is reasonably current.*

Q   What can I do with my old cell phone?

A   *Cell phones are designed to last at least five years, but many of us bow to fashion and upgrade on a yearly basis. Over 100,000,000 cell phones are thrown away each year in Europe alone, of which 80 percent are not recycled. Obviously, the environmental impact of this waste is enormous. You can recycle your old cell phone through charitable organizations, or even your cell service provider. Look online to check out your options.*

40

Four wheels bad

It's a biggie, but ditching your motor will make you happier, healthier, wealthier, and wiser.

If you can't do without your wheels, then at least take action to reduce CO_2 emissions.

Cameron Diaz, Leonardo DiCaprio, and Thandie Newton all have one thing in common, apart from being famous: They ditched their gas-guzzling celeb-mobiles in favor of a low-carbon hybrid car; in their case, the Toyota Prius. Other stars, including George Clooney, are going all electric with models such as the Tesla Roadster.

While Hollywood celebs seem to be embracing the new breed of eco-cars, the rest of us are trailing behind. A hybrid or electric car may be too expensive or not suit our day-to-day needs for various reasons, but there are still things we can look out for when buying a new car.

The most obvious route is to choose the smallest and most fuel-efficient vehicle possible. This will also save money in other running costs. Look for one with the lowest CO_2 emissions of its class.

Many new carmakers are giving plenty of useful information to help you make your choice, such as eco-labels that show its CO_2 figure and estimated annual running

Here's an idea for you...

If you live in a town or city, joining a car club is a great way of cutting down on gas emissions and will save you loads in running costs as well. You only rent the car when you need it, but this can be by the hour, week, month, or longer. Membership gives you access to a pool of cars near your home, which you can book in advance or on the day, and covers insurance, servicing, maintenance, and valeting. Most car clubs are run along very simple lines—you can log in online (or by phone) and reserve your car on the spot. A pin number enables you to drive the car away.

costs, and possibly even its life cycle assessment, which examines the whole impact of the vehicle from factory to final disposal.

Driving more environmentally friendly vehicles can help reduce emissions, improve people's health, and save money.

Manufacturers now produce low-carbon electric, hybrid, and dual-fuel vehicles. Some of these low-carbon vehicles also have financial benefits such as lower tax, cheaper fuel options, and lower running and maintenance costs.

Electric vehicles produce no emissions—CO_2 or toxic emissions—but need to be recharged often and can't travel long distances. But they are great in cities, on set routes, or for short trips.

Hybrid vehicles switch between gas and electricity. Because they use far less gas than traditional vehicles, they produce much lower CO_2 and other emissions. Most big car manufacturers are planning to introduce a hybrid model in the next few years.

LPG vehicles run mainly on LPG (liquid petroleum gas), which produces much lower emissions—about 10–15 percent less CO_2, 75 percent less carbon monoxide, and 85 percent less hydrocarbons—and is much cheaper than unleaded gas.

These aren't the only options. More vehicles are being produced that emit less CO_2 and other pollutants. Car magazines, websites, and government bodies will have useful comparison data.

We should all be walking more. Find out about the benefits in IDEA 28, *A change of sport?*

Try another idea…

ECO-DRIVING

The way you drive your car also has an impact on the environment. If you're eco-savvy, emissions and fuel consumption can be reduced by up to 25 percent.

- Drive off right away rather than letting the engine warm up.
- When the engine is cold, journeys of less than two miles pollute by up to 60 percent more per mile than a hot engine.
- Use higher gears as soon as traffic conditions allow. Minimum emissions happen between 40–60 miles per hour and increase when you drive faster.
- Regular maintenance will reduce emissions.
- Restarting the engine uses less energy than ten seconds of idling, so switch off if in a long line.
- Hard acceleration and sharp braking use more fuel as well as being more dangerous.
- Plan ahead: Choose quiet routes, combine trips, and carpool.
- Don't carry unnecessary weight on the roof or in the trunk.
- Make sure your tires are inflated to the right pressure and reduce greenhouse gas emissions by 5 percent.
- Cut back on onboard electrical devices and air-conditioning to reduce fuel consumption.

"Environmentally friendly cars will soon…become a necessity."
FUJIO CHO, Toyota Motors

Defining idea…

181

How did it go?

Q **What should I look for when I buy a new car?**

A Choose a car with the lowest CO_2 emission levels where possible: small car, small engine usually equals smaller CO_2 emissions. There can also be a big difference in emissions of cars in the same category, so compare before buying. Examine the environmental label, which should be displayed on all new cars in showrooms.

Q **Can you tell me about the new biofuels?**

A Biofuels are made from biological sources such as vegetable oil, and generate far fewer and less harmful emissions than gas or diesel. But there are fears that they may be made from crops that threaten to compete with food production and destroy rainforests, actually releasing more carbon into the atmosphere than is saved. Biogas offers the least environmentally damaging prospect, as it is created from waste material that would otherwise have a negative impact on the land and the atmosphere. Organic materials are broken down by a microbiological activity to produce methane. Other fuels include biodiesel, pure plant oils (PPO), and bioethanol, which is produced by the fermentation of starch, sugar, and cellulose plants. Some cars can run on these biofuels alone; others operate best on a blend with gas or diesel.

41

Work for a better future

Put the squeeze on your workplace—at home or away—and help reduce climate change.

You're bound to spend several hours a day there, so why not make your office as green as you can?

Whether you work alone or with a group of people, at home or in a large organization, the way your office is run can have a massive impact on the environment. Even doing simple things that cost little or nothing can help tackle the big problems, such as the greenhouse effect and climate change.

ENERGY

Most offices today possess a battery of electronic equipment such as photocopiers, printers, and computers, which are essential but use up loads of electricity. Electricity production contributes to global climate change, air pollution, and the consumption of natural resources. So cutting energy use at work means we can help reduce these harmful effects—and save money.

- Use low-energy lightbulbs—they consume 80 percent less energy than normal lightbulbs, providing the same amount of light from a much lower wattage.

- Turn down your heating—if your workplace heating system has thermostatic valves on radiators, use them.
- Switch off all equipment at night—an average-size photocopier left on overnight wastes enough energy to make several thousand copies, while a PC monitor left on overnight could drain enough energy to print several hundred copies!
- Use the natural light from windows to reduce the need for lighting. Keep windows clean and free of files, knickknacks, or large plants, so light can get in.
- Use the energy saving features on equipment, such as automatic standby mode or automatic switch off.

WASTE

By reducing, reusing, and recycling waste from the office we can save money, natural resources, and energy. Remember the three Rs:

- *Reduce.* Cut down on the amount of waste we generate by using both sides of paper. Make sure you use the double-sided function on photocopiers and printers. Only print when necessary and use small font sizes where you can. Use your own mug or glass rather than plastic or polystyrene cups for drinks. Use email rather than messages on paper.

Here's an idea for you...

Don't throw out your empties! Around 90 percent of used-up ink and toner cartridges can be refilled up to eight or ten times, so don't simply trash them when they get to the end of their printing life. When they finally reach the cut-off for refilling you can recycle them, either trading up to new cartridges or selling the empties on for charity. This can be done across all levels, from a tiny home office to huge multinational companies, so tell your boss, family, and friends.

- *Reuse*. Make your own paper pads from scrap paper and when printing draft copies use scrap paper. Printer and photocopier toner cartridges can be recycled and reused. Reuse envelopes for internal circulation and buy envelope reuse labels.
- *Recycle*. Be scrupulous about recycling glass, paper, plastic, metal, and other materials. Ask the local government for advice if necessary.

There is a big market for recycled office products. Find out more about recycling in IDEA 4, *Once more with feeling*.

Try another idea...

PURCHASING

No matter what products you use in the workplace, they will have consumed energy and raw materials during their manufacture.

They also affect the environment in their use and ultimately their disposal. You can reduce this impact through thoughtful purchasing. For example, if buying a photocopier ask the following questions:

- Does it have an Energy Star rating?
- Is it equipped with a standby mode?
- In use, how does its energy consumption compare with other makes?
- Does it have an ozone filter?

"Inspiration comes of working every day."
CHARLES BAUDELAIRE

Defining idea...

Many offices buy and use far more than they actually need, meaning that more resources are consumed than is necessary. There is a lot that can be done to cut down on what is bought and to use what we have more efficiently.

OTHER WAYS TO WORK GREENER

- Plants in the office are a vital step to greening the office, both visually and environmentally. They humidify and purify the air, help deaden noise, and, in open plan offices, act as organic room dividers.
- Take the stairs rather than the elevator—it's healthier and reduces energy use.
- Invest in solar-powered calculators rather than battery operated.
- Avoid disposable products in favor of reuseable items: china cups, metal cutlery, mechanical pencils, refillable pens.
- If you're buying wooden office furniture make sure it is from certified, sustainable sources.
- Use solvent-free correction fluids and paints.
- Choose local products and materials to reduce energy and pollution.
- Avoid overpackaged goods.
- Specify upgradeable PCs.
- Share items in occasional use, e.g., hole punchers.
- Position desks and workstations to make best use of natural light.
- Check for and quickly repair leaks and dripping taps.
- Service heating systems regularly.
- Improve insulation and draft-proofing, and only heat work areas that are being used.
- Reduce lighting levels in areas such as corridors where bright lighting is not required.
- Consider other energy saving measures such as timers and sensors.

Q   My staff want to go green. How can they help?

A   Ask staff to come up with new ideas for improving the office environment, through email or perhaps an Intranet forum discussion group. You could also organize a stationery "amnesty" to reduce demand. A good look at what supplies you've got will make everyone aware of existing stock so you can reorder more accurately.

Q   How can I spread the word?

A   One good way is through your buying power. A green purchasing initiative will help your own environmental performance and influence other organizations and manufacturers. So, develop a green buying policy, for example, buy low-energy appliances where possible, and ask your suppliers to do likewise. When buying office goods always ask if there is a green version. Learn about the different eco labels that are used. Some of these carry unsubstantiated environmental claims, so make sure you know exactly what each label means, and who issues them.

How did
it go?

42

A clean break

Responsible tourism is fine, but when it comes to booking a vacation, how do you sort the green from the greenwash?

There's more to ecotourism than recycling napkins and visits to wildlife parks, so read the small print before you book.

Eco-travel is fast becoming big business, and as green spending power increases so do some travel firms' claims of sustainability.

We've all heard to the term "ecotourism" bandied about, but not everyone knows exactly what it means. Once the preserve of the beard and sandals brigade, these days it is generally agreed that ecotourism—or "sustainable tourism"—involves traveling responsibly to regions in a way that helps protect the environment and benefits the lifestyle of the local people.

Ecotourism can encompass a wide range of features, but you would probably expect it to include accommodation built from local, preferably recycled, materials, fairly paid staff from the immediate area, energy from renewable sources where possible, and water-saving policies. Eco-holidays should have no impact on the natural environment, and should help maintain traditional cultures and customs.

Trips can vary from exclusive, luxurious spa breaks that make use of all the latest environmentally friendly technology to simple walking holidays, camping or staying in adobe huts with local hosts. To some extent you have to sort the wheat from the chaff, as there are a number of travel firms who have jumped on the lucrative green bandwagon with only a nod in the direction of ecological principles.

Here's an idea for you...

Why not skip the beach this year and opt for a conservation break instead? From landscape restoration in Transylvania through wildlife management in Botswana to tree planting in Nepal, there is a project worldwide to suit everyone. You normally have to pay a fee to cover your travel and some expenses, but it goes without saying that these kinds of vacations improve the environment, benefit local communities, and are great for your health and sense of purpose, too.

It's not ecotourism if the resort café simply has fair-trade coffee, includes visits to the homes of the locals, or uses solar power. What you need to look out for are wide-ranging measures that cover the whole experience.

There are hotels, for instance, that are furnished in almost 100 percent recycled material, and invest in efficient technologies that minimize their use of electricity and water. Other travel operators work alongside welfare or conservation charities, offer the opportunity for customers to offset carbon emissions from flights, or set up funding initiatives to benefit local communities directly.

So just how do you sort the green from the greenwash? The best way is to simply ask!

- How do you minimize impact on the local environment?
- How do you build environmental and cultural awareness?

- Do you provide direct financial benefits for conservation?
- Do you provide financial benefits and empowerment for local people?
- How do you fit in with host countries' political, environmental, and social climate?

Booking an eco-vacation is a start, but the way you behave when traveling is just as important, too. Read IDEA 43, *The traveler's footprint*, for more details.

Try another idea…

While you can obviously form your own judgment of a company it would be helpful if there was an international form of classification, an eco star-rating system to help you assess how green travel firms are. At the time of writing such a system doesn't exist, although there are various, more scattered initiatives, which include:

- Green Globe (www.greenglobe.org), a global benchmarking, certification, and improvement system for sustainable travel and tourism.
- The Association of Independent Tour Operators (www.aito.com) has introduced its own responsible tourism star rating system for members.
- The UK's Green Tourism Business Scheme (www.green-business.co.uk) lists more than 1,000 places to stay in England and Scotland and is a member of a European association known as the Voluntary Initiative for Sustainability in Tourism, which is trying to provide a universal certification system.
- The website www.responsibletravel.com provides a good overview of the issues involved and offers a wide range of ecotourism holidays, from holistic centers in the Greek islands to wildlife tours in the Antarctic.
- The Travel Foundation (www.thetravelfoundation.org.uk) also airs the issues— and provides a handy list of the many ways individuals can travel more responsibly.

"Who lives sees much. Who travels sees more."

ARAB PROVERB

Defining idea…

191

How did it go?

Q Does "responsible" travel really make a difference?

A *It depends on the extent of the travel company's commitment to eco-friendly principles. Having organic cotton towels in the bathrooms won't stop climate change but running a whole resort on solar power might help its carbon footprint. And, increasingly, ecotourism vacations involve conservation projects or helping local communities recover after natural disasters, such as flooding or earthquakes. Now that the big travel companies are jumping on the green bandwagon, ecotourism will become even more popular, helping to preserve the world's most threatened regions.*

Q Many of these eco-vacations involve flying long distances—isn't that adding to global warming?

A *Aviation is the fastest growing cause of global warming, although at the moment it accounts for less than 5 percent of carbon dioxide emissions. Yes, we should all fly less, if at all, but there are other benefits to responsible tourism. Around one in ten jobs globally is in tourism, with tourism growing fastest in developing countries, which often can only make a living from their cultures and natural environments. And ecotourism often supports conservation of forests, which absorb carbon dioxide. If you do fly, look into carbon offsetting, where you pay extra to support lower carbon dioxide initiatives to compensate for the carbon dioxide that your flight emits. Although carbon offsetting shouldn't give us carte blanche to keep on flying anywhere we please, it does mitigate emissions. Keep your carbon footprint small through other lifestyle measures too, such as energy conservation at home.*

43

The traveler's footprint

Taking a day trip? Traveling around the world? The message is the same: Your behavior could have a big impact on the local environment.

Get a little bit more out of your travels and give something back to the places you visit and the people you meet.

No matter where your travels take you this year, traveling responsibly maximizes the benefits and minimizes the negative effects of tourism. You can start thinking "low impact" before you go, even if you're not traveling abroad. Plan your route to minimize carbon emissions—go by train and public transportation where possible, rather than driving or flying.

For the flights that you can't avoid, offset the carbon emissions through one of the many carbon balancing programs around. Examples include reforestation programs, providing low-energy lightbulbs to poorer households, or developing community-based hydro-electricity.

If you are using a tour operator or travel agent ask to see their policy for responsible tourism. Make sure it explains how they minimize environmental impact and support the local economy. Find out whether there are local conservation projects that you could visit, and how you could help support them.

OUT AND ABOUT

It sounds obvious, but a lot of people don't do it: show respect for other people's culture and customs. Ask permission before you take photos of people or sensitive buildings. Be careful not to disturb ruins and historic sites. If you hire a local guide you'll discover more about local culture and lives, and they will earn an income.

Here's an idea for you...

Get into the habit of taking a recycled plastic bag for collecting your litter wherever you travel. Our throwaway society has lead to a massive increase in litter. Litter ruins the local landscape, and is a menace to wildlife. Animals and birds can get trapped inside bottles, cans, or bags; choke on plastics and other litter; and suffocate inside plastic bags. They can also get caught up in multi-pack drink can holders, and either choke or be poisoned by eating cigarette butts.

WILDLIFE

One of the pleasures of traveling is the variety of wild plants and shells you will see. These should remain in their natural environment, so don't be tempted to collect any.

Take care not to touch coral reefs and do not feed animals or fish. Wild animals and farm animals can behave unpredictably if you get too close, especially if they're with their young—so give them plenty of space.

LITTER

Litter and leftover food spoil the beauty of the countryside, can be dangerous to wildlife and farm animals, and can spread disease—so take it home with you. In areas where there are no recycling facilities, the less you create, the better. Take a reusable bottle for water, keep packaging down to a minimum, and avoid disposable goods.

WATER AND ENERGY

In many destinations natural resources are precious and local people may not have enough for their own needs. Help out by turning off (or down) heating, air-conditioning, lights, and the TV when you're not using them. Let staff know if you are happy to reuse towels and bed linens rather than having them replaced daily. Monitor the water you're using. If you have to wash in streams or rivers, don't use detergents or other chemicals—go for an eco-soap instead. Use public transportation, rent a bike, or walk when convenient—it's a great way to meet local people on their terms and reduce pollution, too.

PROTECT THE LANDSCAPE

Discover the beauty of the natural environment and take special care not to damage features such as rocks, plants, and trees that are the homes and food for wildlife. In fields where crops are growing, follow paths wherever you can. Use gates, stiles, or gaps in field boundaries—climbing over walls, hedges, and fences can damage them.

Hotter and drier weather conditions recently have made wildfires a problem in some rural areas, and they are devastating to wildlife and habitats as well as to people and property. Don't drop matches or cigarette butts and if you're planning a barbecue make sure it is allowed in that particular area; be sure to extinguish it carefully.

Keep dogs under close control. Don't let your dog scare livestock or disturb nesting birds and other wildlife. Always clean up after your dog—get rid of the mess responsibly and keep your dog wormed regularly to protect it, other animals, and people.

If you've been impressed by any of the landscapes or cultures you've seen on your travels, why not support them with a funding initiative, as outlined in IDEA 49, *Cash, now!*

Try another idea...

"Take only photos, leave only footprints."
POPULAR SAYING

Defining idea...

195

Q Should I give money to beggars?

A *It's best not to give out sweets or money, especially to children. Though begging is the sole source of income for many of the world's poor, giving money to charities can often offer more long-term help to a far greater number of people. Many tour operators support all kinds of charitable initiatives and can suggest ways of supporting the destinations you've visited.*

Q Is it OK to buy local souvenirs?

A *Yes, especially as many communities in tourist destinations depend on their livelihood from selling souvenirs. But don't be tempted to buy products made from genuine ancient artifacts or endangered species. In many countries haggling is the name of the game, but do stop once you have a reasonable price so you don't exploit the poverty and desperation of sellers.*

Q It must be OK to pick up the occasional pebble from the beach. After all, there are millions more!

A *You may think taking the odd pebble, plant, or seashell from the beach is OK, but collectively they help make up the delicate and balanced environment of the coast. Imagine if every visitor were to take away one of these natural "souvenirs," beaches would end up looking naked! Bear in mind, too, that some coasts are protected land, and you can be fined for taking natural items away, even if they look discarded.*

44

Put your money where your mouth is

Carry out a financial health check: Could your money be doing more for the environment?

When it comes to your money, do you let your principles rule your profits?

Ethical financial products have been around in various guises for many years, and recently they have been extended to include investments, bank accounts, insurance, pensions, and mortgages whose management also carries environmental benefits. Other kinds of companies that handle your money, such as phone, TV, and cell phone suppliers, ISPs, and retailers are also going greener. However, ethical (or socially responsible) investment can be very confusing, as there are so many different funds available that claim to be "green." In reality some of these funds are more environmentally friendly than others.

THE GREEN AND NOT-SO-GREEN

You can find out which companies have ethical policies by simply reading information readily found on their websites or company literature. Broadly speaking, a truly ethical company will be one that is not causing damage to the environment, exploiting its workforce by paying low wages, using child labor, or producing products that are harmful or dangerous.

Two sets of criteria—one positive, one negative—identify ethical investments. Positive criteria include:

■ Specific environmental protection practices
■ Pollution control
■ Involvement in conservation and recycling measures
■ Ethical employment practices

Negative criteria include:

■ Environmentally damaging practices
■ Animal exploitation and testing
■ Involvement in supporting oppressive regimes
■ Alcohol, tobacco, gambling, and pornography
■ Involvement in armaments and nuclear weapons manufacture

Here's an idea for you...

Invest thoughtfully, but do get your calculator out before you sign up for a so-called ethical financial product. For example, some banks will make a donation to charities that combat global warming by investing in projects to offset carbon emissions, in return for each mortgage taken out. All well and good. But that doesn't mean it's the best deal—you may release more cash for good causes by shopping around for a cheaper product and donating any savings you make to the charity of your choice. So find out exactly how much the promised amount adds up to before you commit.

Criteria like these are not necessarily fail-safe, and certainly not tailor-made to your particular set of beliefs. For instance, you might be attracted to investing in a bio-technology company that is carrying out groundbreaking research into tuberculosis but is also involved in genetically-modified foods that you might shy away from. You have to decide how to prioritize your principles, otherwise you may end up not investing in any companies at all!

As the World Trade Organization begins to crack down on companies exploiting people, animals, or the environment, companies who don't play the game may well receive negative press and lose customers, meaning they'll start to underperform. Well-run companies with strong ethical principles should be tomorrow's top performers, along with the many companies producing sustainable energy products. So, think long term when you're investing your money.

Use your spending power in another way, to buy greener electricity, in IDEA 15, *Earth, wind, and water.*

Try another idea...

YOUR GREEN MONEY

Look out for service companies in any field who do any of the following:

- Promote sustainable forms of transportation.
- Offer paper-free billing and online statements.
- Participate in tree-planting initiatives to help offset CO_2 emissions.
- Offer mortgage deals based on how ecologically sound/energy-efficient your home is.
- Lenders who will make a payment every year, for as long as you hold your account/mortgage, to charities dedicated to tackling global warming.
- Funds that are used to finance renewable energy plans such as small hydro-electric projects and wind farms.
- Credit cards that allow you to raise money for environmental causes every time you use your plastic.

"If you make money your god, it will plague you like the devil."

HENRY FIELDING

Defining idea...

199

- Deals such as discounts and lower-rate borrowing when you buy certain green energy-saving products or services, such as public transportation tickets.
- Credit and debit cards that can be recycled, or are made from recycled materials.

How did it go?

Q Hate to say it, but don't the "sin stocks" such as tobacco and arms companies offer higher returns for investors than ethical funds?

A In the past ethical funds have underperformed alongside mainstream funds because stocks such as the ones you mention have an alarming habit of being very profitable. But now ethical funds are turning the tables on their ugly sisters. With the green dollar in so much demand, ethical funds are starting to outperform mainstream funds. Check before you invest.

Q I don't think my bank is doing enough for the environment. What can I do?

A If you have a concern about any company that handles your money, write to the chief executive or go to the annual general meeting when the company's board has to face its shareholders and answer questions. You could also join an activist group that adds a communal voice to a concern.

Q Where can I find out more?

A Organizations such as the World Trade Organization and Eiris (the Ethical Investment Research Service) can provide more information about ethical investment. Once you have decided to make an ethical investment it's a good idea to get some independent professional advice.

45
Outside the box

From mosquito nets to mango plantations, your ethical gift to friends and family could have global benefits.

Your carefully chosen eco-gifts are sure to be presents for the future.

Christmas, birthdays, Mother's Day, Valentine's Day, and other special festivals throughout the year all add up to one thing: lots and lots of present buying.

Do we have more money than sense? Sometimes I think so when I see all the trash around that is loosely classed as "gifts." And, all too often, your carefully chosen offering is simply shoved into the back of a closet or drawer.

Now could be the time to finally resolve to ditch some of the wastefulness, and turn instead to gifts that have more long-term benefits to communities and the planet.

Of course there are hundreds of shops and websites dedicated to eco-gifts made from organic cotton, recycled materials, fair-trade products, and even elephant dung, but sometimes it's nice to offer something a little different. Charities such as Oxfam run highly successful stores that sell ethically produced goods, but they also have online stores where instead of buying a tangible present you pay for something that goes to a developing community, while the recipient of your gift gets a certificate or card that represents the donation. They even operate wedding lists!

You can pay for an animal such as a donkey, goat, or yak; a series of school dinners; saplings; and food growing packs. The more generous can splurge on new toilet facilities, gardens, or a whole mango plantation! You could also buy membership to an eco-charity.

For veggie wannabes, an introductory organic fruit and vegetable box is an affordable way of going green, and you can supplement it with chocolate, honey, cheese, and other organic products.

Here's an idea for you...

One practical and eco-friendly gift you could give concerned friends and family is a climate relief pack like the one produced jointly by MoonEstates and the Science Museum in London. The packs offer information about how much CO$_2$ is released by everyday activities, and contain carbon emissions credits, which help to neutralize the gift pack recipient's own carbon footprint. Purchasers of the gift pack will have directly prevented carbon dioxide from being released into the atmosphere by major polluters under the Kyoto Treaty carbon trading plan.

Planting a tree is an awful lot more sustainable than putting a few fresh flowers into water. Organizations such as World Land Trust offer a range of packages from an acre of rainforest to your very own reserve. The Woodland Trust also offers a tree sponsorship plan.

If it's flowers you're after, buy locally produced blooms, or cut the carbon footprint of your bouquet further by sending a virtual version.

From whales to dormice, there's an endangered animal out there that needs your sponsorship. Adopters normally receive a gift pack containing an adoption certificate, a fact sheet about the animal, and sometimes a soft toy version. Most wildlife charities offer this service, and it's especially good for kids.

THE WRAP TRAP

It can be tempting to splurge on cards and wrapping paper, but it doesn't do the planet any favors—your gift wrap was once a tree! You can easily find gift wrap made from recycled paper, and you can reuse your own. Another option is to use aluminum foil, which can be recycled or even reused (after a wash).

Bags and boxes are an alternative to wrapping paper that can be recycled by you and the person you are giving them to. You could reuse specially made gift bags you've received, or bags from nice shops. These can be personalized and the name of the store disguised with scraps of wrapping paper or ribbons.

Greenest of all, dispense with wrapping altogether: hide presents and make a treasure hunt; wrap something in a pretty scarf or piece of fabric scrap; or conceal it in a bag, box, or tin, maybe found in a local secondhand shop.

Tie up with reusable fabric ribbons, a string of beads, or even plain string. Use baubles instead of bows, or even hair accessories. These can then be hung on the tree at Christmas.

Make your own cards from recycled paper or send e-cards.

Buying gifts from green charities is one way to be planet friendly but what's stopping you from raising the cash yourself? Look out for fund-raising tips in IDEA 49, *Cash now!*

Try another idea...

"Liberality consists less in giving a great deal than in gifts well-timed."

JEAN DE LA BRUYERE,
French essayist

Defining idea...

203

How did
it go?

Q I'm not sure a goat or tree planting gift would work with my nieces and nephews. What other green gifts would suit a teenager?

A   *If they are into wildlife conservation, you could buy them the chance to be a zookeeper for the day—a plan offered by many zoos to over-sixteens that makes for an exciting present. Of course you could just be ultra-practical and buy a solar-powered iPod recharger or an LED flashlight, ethically made fashion accessories, or funky wind-up radios. Simpler still, fair-trade chocolate or cotton products such as T-shirts are both widely available from large retailers. Many green charities such as WWF sell their own range of natural toiletries without harmful chemicals, good for both boys and girls.*

Q Is there anything a little more personal yet still green I could give as a present?

A   *Making your own gifts is a lovely, personal way to celebrate a special day. Plant bulbs or houseplants in glass bowls of pebbles or pretty containers; make your own chutney, jam, or wine in cute jars and bottles and labeled with recycled paper. Even a homemade cake is great and invariably a welcome, ecologically friendly gift. Accompany it with a homemade card, perhaps with paper you've made yourself from recycled materials and pressed wildflowers.*

46

Way to go

We all have to shuffle off this mortal coil at some point, so plan in advance for a greener funeral.

Bamboo caskets? Freeze-dried remains? The funeral business is keeping apace with the voracious demand for all things eco.

It may seem ghoulish to be planning funerals in advance, but a growing number of people, young and old, are hoping for an eco-friendly death. After all, if caring about the environment is an important part of your life, what could be more fitting than an ending that embraces the natural cycle of death, decay, and new growth?

On the face of it, cremation may seem appealing—the notion of a clean, hot fire that leaves little residue combined with the high cost of burial plots has made cremation a cheaper and more attractive option. However, there is a not-so-green side to cremation. Wooden coffins are burned, releasing dioxin, hydrochloric acid, hydrofluoric acid, sulphur dioxide, and carbon dioxide into the atmosphere, using large amounts of timber.

Ovens in crematoria burn for around an hour and a half per body, at temperatures of up to 2000 degrees F, consuming the same amount of energy as an average person would use at home in a month in the process. As they burn any mercury in fillings go up in smoke, too, contaminating air, water, and soil. And dioxins released from crematoria are linked with illnesses that include cancer.

There are a few green steps you can take—for instance, asking whether the crematorium has installed filters that help remove mercury emissions. Most crematoria now accept a cardboard coffin and some even offer a discount as less energy is used.

If you hate the thought of cardboard, you could consider a coffin cover: typically a traditional oak casket sourced from sustainably managed trees, and an inner coffin made of cardboard or recycled composite material. Only the inner coffin is paid for and cremated; the outer casket is owned by the funeral director and reused.

Ashes can be stored in urns made from bamboo, reed, wood, glass, and ceramic.

Here's an idea for you...

For your own peace of mind, it's worth drawing up your own eco-funeral plan now. This will ensure you get exactly what you want, and will also save your family or friends from having to second-guess your preferences later on. A plan will also help you budget; you'll be paying at today's prices! Once you've found the right funeral provider, they should send you a written confirmation with all your requirements set out. Make sure any money you pay is underwritten.

GOING UNDERGROUND

Burial can be a greener option, so long as you go about it the right way; for instance, in choosing the right coffin.

The majority of coffins are made of a wooden veneer pasted onto chipboard, which contains formaldehyde that soaks into the ground over time.

There are a number of eco-designs on the market made from natural materials without harmful chemicals, such as biodegradable papier-mache made out of recycled paper, bamboo, wicker, seagrass, and willow.

A WOODLAND SETTING?

If you've opted for burial and chosen your coffin, the next step is to choose a location.

Whether you're planning a wake or christening, there are loads of ideas for green celebrations in IDEA 51, *An eco-friendly party*.

Try another idea...

Urban cemeteries are running out of space, which means that managed woodland burial sites are becoming increasingly popular.

Woodland burial sites are kept as natural and wild as possible in order to promote bio-diversity, and the land is preserved from development. Graves are usually unmarked, although a memorial tree or wildflowers can take the place of a headstone.

A key attraction of a funeral at a natural burial ground is the freedom offered to choose the format of the service. They are suitable for the religious and the secular alike, and the mourners can take all the time they need to say goodbye. Bodies buried in natural sites are not embalmed, to avoid harmful chemicals polluting the ground.

It is likely that natural burial will eventually overtake cremation, currently used in 70 percent of funerals. As nature takes its course, graveyards will probably evolve to resemble wooded parkland, with wildlife roaming free, communal picnic areas, and nature trails.

You can usually bury bodies on private land with permission of the owner (handy if you happen to know a sympathetic farmer), although there are rules about how and where—contact your local authority for more information. Bear in mind, though, that a willow coffin decomposing in your back garden may be green but won't exactly add to property values if you decide to sell!

"I intend to live forever. So far, so good!"

ANONYMOUS

Defining idea...

How did it go?

Q   **Can't bodies simply be freeze-dried?**

A   *In theory, yes, though in practice not all countries allow it. But in Sweden, for example, a radical new technique called promession involves freeze-drying corpses in liquid nitrogen. The water that makes up the majority of a human being evaporates and the resulting powder can be composted in cornstarch coffins. Of course creating liquid nitrogen uses energy, but the process is gradually becoming more efficient. It is likely that laws will change in the near future to allow the promession technique to be used more widely.*

Q   **Services with the word "eco" seem to come with a higher price—is that the case with eco-funerals?**

A   *Thanks to cheaper burial plots and materials, the average price of a wood-land burial is only around a third of the cost of a conventional one. Another plus point is that often part of the cost goes toward an environmental charity. Some crematoria offer discounts for cardboard coffins as they use less energy. But like anything, it may pay to get more than one quote.*

Q   **How can I find a natural burial ground?**

A   *Try an organization such as The Natural Death Centre (www.naturaldeath .org.uk/usa_and_canada), which offers advice and list of members. Feel free to ask green funeral providers questions: What stops the burial ground from being sold or even leased to other people, e.g., developers in the long term? Is there a deed or trust document protecting the cemetery from com-mercial exploitation in the future? What happens if the current owner dies, sells their interest, or simply moves on?*

47

Get involved

Feeling green but lonely? Don't fret, there are sure to be like-minded people in your neighborhood—all you have to do is find them!

Whether you want to campaign, volunteer, or learn something new, joining or starting a local group will give you people power.

Warning: Turning eco is highly addictive. Once the green bug bites, you'll want to get into the whole environmental thing in more depth, meeting other like-minded eco-warriors, finding out more information, and discovering how your local community is helping to change things.

The first thing you could do is head down to your local library or log onto your town's website and find out if there are any environmental groups in your neighborhood. These could be anything from local conservation volunteers to die-hard campaigners—it's up to you how far you want to go.

There is sure to be a branch near you, and you can join in every once in a while or every week—the choice is yours. Often, there's no need to book in advance—just show up at the meeting point on the day.

Here's an idea for you...

Find out if your neighborhood runs a local skill-swapping service, and if it doesn't, then start one yourself! Babysitting, plumbing, typing, web design, hiring of tools and equipment, gardening, or dog walking: you name it, your neighborhood is sure to offer it in some shape or form. Sometimes called LETS—Local Exchange Trading Systems—these community-based networks allow people to exchange all kinds of goods and services with one another, without spending a penny. You can set up a system of community credits, bypassing the need for direct exchanges. People earn credits by providing a service, and can then spend the credits on whatever is offered by others in the system. That way, you bypass the whole consumer culture.

Tasks vary from tree planting to dry stone walling, footpath construction to creating wildlife habitats. You don't need to be an eco-expert, either—project leaders will show you the ropes and you're free to work at your own pace.

You'll make new friends, get some fresh air, exercise, and help your local environment.

Normally, groups focus on just one or two measures—for example, heating, electricity, car, and plane travel. The groups help members calculate their individual carbon footprints, and agree on a target, perhaps 4,500 kilograms of CO_2 per person.

Apart from helping you get your carbon footprint down, it's a marvelous way of meeting new people and widening your knowledge of the whole climate change topic. Often groups invite expert guests along to talk about their fields. In a similar initiative, whole towns and communities are swapping over to fair-trade goods.

Not everybody wants to belong to a group or organization, and there are many other less formal ways of tapping into your local community. Why not arrange a swap party, for instance, with people you work with, your children's friends' parents, neighbors, or community groups? Swap parties are the eco-friendly way to get new books, clothes, and CDs without contributing to a consumer drive. The idea is that everyone brings things along to the party that they don't want anymore—computer software, homemade produce, tools, old school textbooks, bottles of wine—it could be absolutely anything. Anything left over can be sold (with the money going to an environmental cause) or donated to charity.

Feeling more committed? Then why not take things a step further, as outlined in IDEA 52, *Eureco! You're getting there.*

Try another idea...

You can do the swap thing online, too, through networks such as Freecycle.com and Craigslist (www.craigslist.org), who have local groups all over the world. Here you can swap your junk, and also find out about carpooling groups, trade swaps, and even accommodation exchanges.

It doesn't have to be tangible items that you exchange. Many local communities operate trading groups where members exchange their goods and services with one an other without payment.

"If we do not change our direction, we are likely to end up where we are headed."
CHINESE PROVERB

Defining idea...

How did
it go?

Q   **I'd like to join a local environmental group but my neighborhood
doesn't seem to have one. Any ideas?**

A   *There are probably lots of people in your area who feel the same way, so
why not start one up yourself? If you're not sure how to go about it, large
organizations such as Friends of the Earth offer lots of advice and information on starting up a local branch, from fund-raising ideas to posters and
DVD loans.*

Q   **I work full-time and don't really have time to attend a group
regularly. But I'd like to do something.**

A   *If you can't commit to a local group, one way of belonging to a community
is through an online group such as Greenpeace, which is developing a thriving community of online activists and making it easier for those who want
to get involved to do so. You can comment on blogs, help get the word out
through social networking sites, and stay better informed through its RSS
feeds. And all without moving from your desk!*

Q   **I—very guiltily—drive into town every weekday for work. Should
I offer someone local the chance to carpool?**

A   *Of course—if others are driving, too, it's the perfect way to reduce harmful
emissions and you'll have the benefit of company and perhaps a contribution toward fuel, too.*

48

Try a low-carb diet

We've all got one, and most of us have a bigger one than we ought to. Yes, our carbon footprint is a key indicator of just how green we really are.

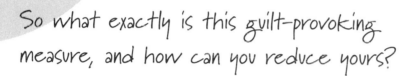

So what exactly is this guilt-provoking measure, and how can you reduce yours?

A couple of years ago, few had even heard the phrase "carbon footprint." But now we're all fast becoming carbon literate, if not yet neutral.

A carbon footprint is the measure of the total amount of greenhouse gases released into the atmosphere as a result of things we do in our everyday lives such as travel, shopping, washing, even watching TV! Your footprint is made up of two parts: the direct or primary footprint; and the indirect or secondary footprint.

The primary footprint measures our direct emissions of CO_2 from the burning of fossil fuels including domestic energy and transport, e.g., car and plane journeys.

The secondary footprint measures indirect CO_2 emissions from the whole life cycle of products we use from manufacture through to eventual breakdown.

A carbon footprint is measured in tons per year, and numerous websites can help you figure out yours, such as www.carbonneutral.com and www.carbonfootprint.com.

Given the plight of the planet, if you figured out what might be an acceptable carbon footprint for the entire globe and then divided it by the global population, you might come up with a figure of about one ton per person.

Oh dear. It goes without saying that in the pampered West our individual carbon footprint is a tad larger. For example, the average US carbon footprint is nearly 20 tons, while each Chinese person has a footprint of around 3.2 tons and the average Indian emits 1 ton.

Here's an idea for you...

Gather together the information you need before you go online to estimate your carbon footprint. You'll need to know how much gas, electricity, or other fossil fuels you've used over a year. If you own a car, you'll need to know the mileage and model. Then think back to your vacations, and any regular commutes you do to roughly figure out your year's worth of travel. When you key this information into the calculator it should convert it into a figure that shows your carbon emissions in tons per year.

It's pretty obvious that the poorer a person is, the less carbon they emit—which doesn't bode well for the future when you consider the rate of economic growth in countries such as China and India!

But everyone can cut their carbon footprint. Although individual actions can't possibly have the impact that reducing aviation fuel use and power station emissions would have, every little bit helps.

For instance, you could save 2 kilograms of carbon for every journey under three miles where you walk and don't use the car, and 30 kilograms by switching the power off in your house at night.

HOW TO SHRINK YOUR PRIMARY FOOTPRINT...

- Don't go by air.
- Sign up to a renewable energy provider.
- Insulate and install solar water heating.
- Use public transportation.
- Carlpool.

If you're shocked by the size of your carbon footprint, find out about getting it down in IDEA 52, *Eureco! You're getting there.*

Try another idea...

...AND YOUR SECONDARY

Don't buy items that produce high emissions in manufacturing or delivery, such as:

- Bottled water, especially from abroad.
- Food and drink from far distances—buy local or grow your own.
- Meat, especially red meat.
- Clothes from far-off lands.
- Highly packaged items.

CARBON OFFSETTING

Carbon offsetting aims to reduce the impact of carbon dioxide emissions from everyday activities such as driving cars, heating homes, and flying. A carbon offset provider can calculate the emissions you produce and then pay for them through a donation to a project that reduces carbon by the equivalent amount.

"Before you finish eating your breakfast this morning you've depended on half the world."
MARTIN LUTHER KING JR.

Defining idea...

215

Energy efficiency initiatives include installing energy saving devices in houses; renewable energy projects such as wind farms; or tree-planting initiatives that can take carbon dioxide out of the atmosphere.

However, carbon offsetting is not the panacea we'd all like. There is a tendency to think that you can simply buy your way out of the problem of rising carbon emissions, and some environmental campaigners are worried that offsetting discourages people from cutting greenhouse gases in the first place.

Still, if you do want to offset—and surely doing something is better than doing nothing—make sure the offset provider conforms to the government's gold standard (www.cdmgoldstandard.org), which adheres to the Kyoto Protocol on climate change.

Still, offsetting only accounts for a fraction of all emissions produced. Long term we need to radically cut our emissions rather than mitigate them.

Q **Can't I just offset my carbon by sponsoring a few trees?**

How did it go?

A *Plant a tree and save the world, right? Well, not exactly—do your research before you get digging. Trees are fab, we all know that, but some of the large-scale planting projects may not be quite as green as they're made out to be. Many environmentalists fear that they can damage the environment and livelihoods in developing countries, especially where there is no variety in the species of trees being planted. Buying forestry offsets isn't reducing your dependence on fossil fuels, which is what is needed to address climate change. So, it still means you have to cut back on your energy usage.*

Q **What is the single biggest thing I can do to reduce my carbon footprint?**

A *It depends on your lifestyle, but there are a few surefire winners: ditch the car or change to a cleaner model, don't fly, buy fewer goods, insulate your home, and save energy.*

Q **Who can pay to offset and at what cost?**

A *Anyone can offset emissions, but it tends to be people in developed countries investing in poorer countries. The prices vary depending on the amount of CO_2 in question. Offsetting flights has been especially popular, in part because of the relative ease of knowing how much CO_2 has been released.*

49

Cash, now!

Creating a sustainable planet for the future costs money, and you can do your part by fund-raising.

The mend of the world is nigh! So long as the funding keeps on coming...

There are hundreds of different ecological campaign groups out there, and they tend to have one thing in common: money. Or, rather, a lack of it. It takes massive resources to do the work that many of them set out to do, whether it's protecting endangered animal species, research into climate change, or planting new areas of rainforest. Many organizations rely on donations, so any contribution you can make is more than welcome.

Of course donating what you can, when you can is great, but you could take it a step further and actively raise money for the eco project of your choice.

HOW YOU CAN RAISE MONEY

Before you hit the streets with your buckets, tickets, or whatever, check what legal and health and safety rules apply in your city or town first.

Some of the best ideas are the simplest; for instance, a sponsored walk or bike ride. Or give up something you would really miss, like chocolate, meat, beer, or TV and get people to sponsor you for each day that you manage to go without.

Here's an idea for you...

Create your own fund-raising web page and watch your donations grow! Global organizations such as World Land Trust and Friends of the Earth can help you raise money online through an event such as a sponsored marathon, bike ride, trek, or anniversary celebration. Using a simple template, you choose a web address for your page, write a title and a message, and add a photo if you like. You can then email the address of your page to everyone you know. They donate online by credit or debit card and the money you raise is paid into your chosen charity's bank account.

Your home can be put to good use; for instance, you could get together with friends and hold a mini concert. Invite people to sing songs, play an instrument, recite poems, or tell jokes; get all your friends, family, and neighbors to come along, and charge them a small entrance fee.

Get the kids involved, too. Ask them to help neighbors with small tasks such as car washing, shopping, or dog walking in return for donations, or get them to hold a sponsored silence, cake sale, recycled-fashion show, disco, or other event at their school. Another way children can help is by packing shoppers' bags (recycled!) in supermarkets—with the manager's permission, of course—while you shake the bucket.

OTHER IDEAS

- Pub quizzes, karaoke, raffles, and tournaments.
- Auction goods on eBay.
- Organize a bring-and-buy, garden plant, organic produce, or yard sale.
- Ask your boss if you can have a paid-for dress-down day.
- Find out about matched funding from your employers.
- Host a murder mystery or haunted weekend.
- Organize an auction for skills and services.

- Run a bowling, football, or Ultimate Frisbee competition.
- Take a fine box into work and ask colleagues to donate their small change as penalties during a "give up swearing/tea/coffee" week.
- Go green. Get sponsored to dress in green all day or hold a green dinner party, making sure that everything is fair-trade or organic.
- Run a sweepstakes among friends and family, e.g., football or horse racing, and split the proceeds between the winner and charity.
- Take part in a sponsored parachute jump, expedition, mountain climbing, or sailing event.
- Cycle or walk to work for a month and donate the usual cost of your travel.

Is your own money doing as much for the environment as it could? Find out in IDEA 44, *Put your money where your mouth is.*

Try another idea…

FUND-RAISING TIPS

- Find out about any possible government grants.
- Simple fund-raising ideas work best, so stick to ideas you can do fairly easily.
- Keep any costs to a minimum.
- Persuade friends, family, and contacts to join in.
- Plan ahead—how much money do you want to raise, what for, when, how, and who is responsible for what?
- Try a variety of different fund-raising activities so you don't depend on just one or two sources of income.
- Shout about your event, and get all the publicity you can.
- Say a big thank-you to all involved and publicize how much was raised.

"The gap in our economy is between what we have and what we think we ought to have."

PAUL HEYNE, economist

Defining idea…

221

How did it go?

Q   I'd like to go on a sponsored field trip. Where do I start?

A   *One of the best places to start is Earthwatch (www.earthwatch.org), which runs more than 130 expeditions all over the world—from monitoring Nile crocodiles in Botswana to looking at the impact of climate change on gray whale populations in Mexico and Canada. You have to pay a fee for these, since bodies such as Earthwatch need your cash. The good news is that there are all kinds of ideas for getting grants and fund-raising available, from sponsored abseiling to hosting a zebra-themed party.*

Q   I don't really have time to join in fund-raising activities. Is there any other way of helping?

A   *One of the easiest ways to raise money for eco-charities is through paid-for recycling programs. Cell phones and ink-jet and laser printer cartridges can often be sold on, so if you work in an office persuade your boss to let you have these when they are used up for the charity of your choice.*

Q   Can I leave money to an environmental cause in my will?

A   *Once you've set aside what you want for family and friends, making a will is a good opportunity to make a donation to your favorite charity, and in most cases should be exempt from tax. Ask your lawyer to help you draw it up so that your bequests are crystal clear and legal.*

50

An awfully green adventure

Swap theme parks for green parks and clothes shopping for bird spotting with a low-cost, low-carbon day out for the whole family.

Take the kids on a day out where the only energy you burn is your own!

How come days out with the kids always seem to involve long, hot journeys in cars that mysteriously end up full of fast-food cartons, candy wrappers, and empty plastic bottles?

But it doesn't have to be that way. For a start, you could go by train or bus, far more eco-friendly forms of transportation than a car. You'll probably get to see more of the countryside, and as you can usually get family travel discounts it can end up being cheaper, too. You could even just walk or cycle somewhere local. Even the smallest or quietest neighborhood has its eco-secrets to reveal, whether it's an ancient pond full of fascinating creatures or a patch of long grass where you can hunt for mini beasts.

Of course there are endless alternative technology centers, biodomes, wildlife centers, and the like to visit, but you could also create your own agenda. It's good for children to learn that a great day out doesn't have to involve huge sums of money, and in fact some of the nicest places are absolutely free!

Here's an idea for you...

Leave the car behind and have a day out by public transportation and foot. Plan a trip with points of interest along the way—a hill for kite flying, a park or woodland, a ruin, a waterfall, or a beach. Canals, old railway lines, waterside walks, and nature trails are good venues in both town and country. Get the kids to note features such as plants and animals, colorful rocks, churches, and farms. Keep any walking doable for their age, and build in escape routes in case you need to bail out. Allow time for breaks, take a picnic or include a visit to a family-friendly restaurant or café.

SEA-LIFE SPOTTING

The coast is an ideal place to appreciate the pleasures of the natural world. You'll be able to spot wildlife such as gulls, ducks, otters, seals, dolphins, porpoises, and even whales, although you may have to join a boat trip for some of them. Remember to take a good pair of binoculars. You can also take part in an organized beach cleanup, helping to tackle the growing problem of litter.

WIND FARMS

Some wind farms are open to the public and have visitor centers and viewing platforms. But even if they aren't, they are often sited near public ground and it is fascinating to go up close to these huge, white windmills and get a feeling for how much energy they produce.

SPONSORED EVENTS

Get some fresh air and exercise and raise some cash for your favorite eco-charity with a sponsored walk, cycle, or swim. Ask friends and relatives for donations and pick a route that is easy for the whole family. You could plan your own event, or join one of the many across the country. When you've finished you'll all have a real sense of achievement.

CONSERVATION

Many conservation organizations run one-day conservation tasks all over the United States. Tasks vary from tree planting to dry stone walling, footpath construction to creating wildlife habitats. It's the ideal way to make friends, get some fresh air, exercise, and help your local environment.

NATURE TRAIL

Younger children enjoy having a simple task, so give them a list of ten things you're likely to come across on a local walk. Include easy-to-spot wildflowers, leaf skeletons, empty snail shells, or round pebbles. You don't have to take what you find, you can just check them off a list or snap them with a camera.

Or go on a mini beast safari. Find a patch of long grass and a couple of nets. Carefully sweep the nets through the grass a few times and then examine what you have caught before releasing them. Expect to find ladybugs, moths, dragonflies, butterflies, grasshoppers, and caterpillars.

ORGANIC FARMS

Take the kids to see where food really comes from with a trip to a working organic farm. They'll be able to watch (and maybe even help with) cows being milked, eggs being collected, and crops being planted or harvested. Younger children may be able to feed piglets, goats, and lambs. Or visit a "pick your own" farm.

Get ideas on how to raise your children the green way in **IDEA 37, *Right from the start*.**

Try another idea...

"Money is not required to buy one necessity of the soul."
HENRY DAVID THOREAU, writer and philosopher

Defining idea...

How did
it go?

Q   There's not much going on where I live. What's an easy, cheap, green day out with two young children?

A   *If you have a park near you, why not take them pond dipping? You don't need lots of special equipment, just a small net or glass jar. The most important tools you have are your eyes—sit or stand still beside your wildlife pond and just watch. You will be amazed what you can see—newts rising to the surface, wild animals coming to the pond to drink, and colorful dragonflies swooping over the pond. When you dip, don't hold any of the creatures with your fingers and make sure you always keep them in water before returning them.*

Q   My children aren't really interested in the environment. Where could I take them to open their minds?

A   *Why not be adventurous and take your children to the woods for the day? Give them a task such as building a den using only the materials that the wood provides, and ask them to identify possible foods, such as berries, leaves, or nuts—but don't let them eat them unless you're absolutely sure, of course. Children enjoy living "wild," and it will give them a chance to get close to nature. If you plan to camp or light a fire, find out about any restrictions by phoning the local authority first.*

An eco-friendly party

Send out e-cards, get your guests to walk or cycle, and then crack open the organic fizz: It's green party time!

Can a party be high energy yet low carbon? Sure, with a little forward planning.

Whether you're hosting a wedding for hundreds or a small, exclusive dinner party, your celebration's green credentials don't just stop at the salads. First off, you'll be choosing the location. Have your party at home if there's room and it's convenient for others, but otherwise choose a venue close to where the majority of your guests live. This will help cut down on the environmental costs associated with travel. Support a location or a nonprofit organization dedicated to green causes: parks, museums, or retreat centers, for instance. Encourage your guests to come by public transportation, or help them with setting up carpools.

Next, you'll be sending out invites. Skip the pretty paper variety and choose e-cards as a more ecologically sound option. Or, if you prefer to commit yourself to paper, make it the recycled kind.

Now, the menu. Don't be tempted to fill up a cart at the nearest supermarket. Instead, visit a local organic farm or farmer's market to stock up on pesticide- and hormone-free goodies. If you're on a budget, try to prepare most of the food

Help your guests to be low carbon with a gift of a low energy lightbulb to help counteract some of the energy used in traveling to your party. If they are coming from far and wide, they'll be generating large quantities of carbon dioxide, which contributes to climate change. But get them to replace a conventional lightbulb with a low energy equivalent, and they'll be saving energy elsewhere. Also, encourage them to come on public transportation or by bike, or share cars.

yourself instead of buying premade, heavily packaged snacks. Rope in friends and family to help if cooking isn't your thing, or just keep it really simple. Finger food is ideal as it cuts out the need for crockery and cutlery—so no washing up or disposable stuff needed!

Buying local products also means they've had to travel only a short distance (versus thousands of miles) to get to your house—which obviously means fewer freighting miles.

Treat your guests to organic wines, juices, and spirits, locally produced where possible, and you'll be getting them merry without the nasty additives found in many drinks and helping to support ecologically minded farmers, vintners, and producers.

When it comes to place settings, use what stuff you've already got. Carry out a crockery and cutlery audit, and scour your home for dishes you may have hidden away. Borrow whatever extras you need rather than buying more. Rent glasses from supermarkets or wine merchants instead of using plastic ones. If you insist on using disposable glassware and plates, buy the kind made from recycled or sustainable materials, e.g., bamboo, corn resin, or sugarcane stalk, or items labeled "biodegradable" or "100% recycled content."

"You know you are getting old when the candles cost more than the cake."
BOB HOPE

Use your imagination when it comes to odds and ends that will add a finishing touch to your décor: centerpieces, table decorations, and placemats. Check out markets and second-hand shops. As long as you wash them in hot water, you are getting something unique and doing your part to create less trash.

Once the party's over you'll need to clean up. Find out about greener ways to a sparkling home in IDEA 6, *Clean but green*.

Try another idea...

If the party is to be held outside and the temperatures drop, don't even think about getting out a patio heater. They are one of the most environmentally unfriendly party accessories you could have, literally heating up the atmosphere. Turn up the music and get people dancing instead!

If it's a kids' party and you're expecting to give away party bags, make them biodegradable, or use pretty scarves to wrap party treats in. Be careful with balloons as they can damage wildlife if allowed to escape, and don't use the helium variety as they don't biodegrade. Look out for eco-paper balloons made of traditional Japanese papers and coated with polyvinyl alcohol, which is soluble in water.

Once your friends have left, sort out any trash and make sure you recycle as much as you can—bottles, cans, packaging, etc.—and give away leftover food rather than just throw it away.

Finally, it's cleanup time, and the chance for you to get on down with plenty of hot water, white wine vinegar, and washing soda rather than toxic chemical cleaners. Use washable, reusable micro cloths, not disposable paper towels, and trash what you must in biodegradable garbage bags.

"Life is a party. You join in after it's started and leave before it's finished."
ELSA MAXWELL, celebrated hostess

Defining idea...

229

Q I'm a fan of fairy lights, but how can I light my party atmospherically without using electricity?

A Cut down on electricity and create a romantic and flattering glow by placing lit candles everywhere. Use soy or beeswax candles, which, unlike petroleum-based paraffin candles, won't emit toxic, sooty fumes. If that sounds complicated, get your hands on some plug-in LED lighting, which comes in pretty colors and is very energy efficient. Use solar lighting outside.

Q What can I use for eco-friendly decorations?

A Make your own decorations out of recycled paper, leaves and berries from the garden, silk flowers, or colorful scarves. Brighten up your home with organic plants, which will also help clear the air of carbon dioxide, and pump in more oxygen. Then give them away at the end and ask guests to plant them outdoors. Buy fair-trade flowers or gather wildflowers, or fill a bowl with colorful fruits.

Q Any ideas for party bags?

A What about giving organic chocolate or small jars of local honey from your local farmers' market? Or you could make a charitable donation to an eco-charity, plant trees in your guests' names, or give a small envelope of wildflower seeds to each person.

Eureco! You're getting there

Consider yourself to be a fully paid-up member of the eco-club? Then take the plunge and commit to a change in lifestyle.

The planet's a tad sickly, but with some TLC from people like you, its prognosis is optimistic.

Even the least media savvy individual must now be aware that planet Earth is in a bit of a mess. And most of us are waking up to the fact that it's not going to get better on its own. The message is getting through loud and clear: We all need to *do something*. Now!

Most of us are now taking steps such as saving energy, flying and driving less, eating organic, and cutting back on water. But could we be doing more?

It's a challenge when we live in such a consumer-led society. For instance, it's all very well buying eco-products, or using your credit card to donate to environmental causes, but the goods you're buying still have to be manufactured, which in turn means producing carbon dioxide and waste.

It's probably no exaggeration to say we have become a generation of shopaholics, bombarded by advertising that persuades us that the more we consume, the better our lives will be.

We shop for fun, status, and self-identity. But our obsessive consumerism is putting enormous pressure on the planet. It simply may not be enough to buy more carefully—what it probably comes down to is buying less!

And if you think that some developing nations are also eagerly waiting for the chance to have a bite of the consumer apple, what will happen when a few billion more people become consumers with the same spending power as the West?

One of the most important mantras to someone who cares about the planet is "Reduce, reuse, recycle."

- Buy less. Reduce unnecessary waste by avoiding pointless purchases. Items that rarely get used can be borrowed or shared with others.
- Buy products that can be reused, to reduce waste.
- Buy products with little packaging.
- Sell or give away unwanted items.
- Buy nontoxic products whenever possible.
- Think before you throw away. Many items that you would normally consider trash could be used for other purposes.
- Recycle whatever you can.

Here's an idea for you...

No local environmental groups in your area? So start your own! Most big eco-organizations offer support, resources, and guidance to people wanting to set up a local branch—all you need is a few like-minded and energetic individuals. And if you're stuck on how to kick off your first meeting, arrange a screening of Al Gore's *An Inconvenient Truth* (but check out the premises' licensing rule first). This hard-hitting film discusses the potentially catastrophic outcome of global warming and can be borrowed from libraries or national campaign groups. It's sure to generate debate among viewers and get them motivated.

GET TO KNOW LABELS

Obviously simply buying less is the aim, but when you do shop, buy more carefully. Learn what labels mean: for instance, you've got fair-trade, low-energy appliance logos, organic certification, the flower symbol awarded to goods and services which meet strict criteria to minimize the impacts of consumer products on the environment. More certified goods are coming onto the market, so keep up with changes in consumer law.

If you believe there's strength in numbers, it's worth making contact with other like-minded greenies. Touch base in IDEA 47, *Get involved*.

Try another idea…

TAKE RESPONSIBILITY

It's all too easy to blame environmental damage on far-away countries or politicians who don't seem to be doing enough, but one important step to making a change is recognizing that you—yes you!—are responsible for your own little bit of pollution, whether it's carbon dioxide, chemicals you flush down the sink, or leftover household waste. Make an effort to reduce, reuse, and recycle and you'll cut back that impact.

MAKE A COMMITMENT

Why not commit to making a real difference by setting yourself some targets? You could aim to reduce your carbon emissions by 20 percent, recycle at least half of your waste, cut your car usage by a third, or simply reduce your fuel bills by 10 percent. Having a concrete target makes it easier to see the difference you're really making.

"The future belongs to those who prepare for it today."

MALCOLM X

Defining idea…

How did it go?

Q I think I'm doing my best for the planet, but will my actions really make a difference?

A   *If you bear in mind that in some countries nearly half of the carbon dioxide emissions, the main greenhouse gas which causes climate change, come from the things we do every day, it's easy to see the difference individuals and households could make. But it is a case of critical mass—the more people who join in, the stronger the effect!*

Q Are politicians doing enough?

A   *Now there's a sixty-four-million-dollar question! Who knows what is enough? But if you don't think they are, get pestering! Write a letter, send an email, or join a campaign that helps you get in touch with the relevant congressperson and provides an email template.*

Q I've got the measure of my carbon footprint. Is there anything else I can calculate to reduce my impact on the environment?

A   *Being green isn't just about climate change—pollution, for instance, is also a big factor. One thing you could do is try to reduce your "toxic splash," the number of synthetic chemicals flushed down drains every day, contained in household products such as toiletries and cleaning materials. These chemicals run into our water system and can damage our health and environment.*

Brilliant resources

ACTION, CONSERVATION, AND INFORMATION GROUPS

Climate Crisis: www.climatecrisis.net
Earthwatch Institute: www.earthwatch.org
Environmental Defense: www.environmentaldefense.org
Friends of the Earth: www.foe.org
Greenpeace: www.greenpeace.org
Natural Resources Defense Council: www.nrdc.org
Sierra Club: www.toowarm.org
TreeHugger: www.treehugger.com
World Wildlife Fund: www.worldwildlife.org

CARS

American Council for an Energy-Efficient Economy: www.greenercars.org
City Car Share: www.citycarshare.org
eRideshare: www.erideshare.com
Flexcar: www.flexcar.com
Green Vehicle: www.epa.gov/greenvehicle
Hybrids.com: www.hybrids.com
Zipcar: www.zipcar.com

ECO-CONSUMERISM

Good Gifts Catalogue: www.goodgifts.org
Heifer International: www.heifer.org
NRDC Great Green Gift-Giving Guide: www.nrdc.org/cities/living/ggift
Sweat Shop Watch: www.sweatshopwatch.org

ENERGY/CARBON SAVING

Carbon Fund: www.carbonfund.org
Fight Global Warming: www.fightglobalwarming.com
Green-E: www.green-e.org

Live Neutral: www.liveneutral.org
Native Energy: www.nativeenergy.com
TerraPass: www.terrapass.com

FUNERALS

Memorial Ecosystems: www.memorialecosystems.com
The Natural Death Centre: http://naturaldeath.org.uk/usa_and_canada.html

GARDENING/FLOWERS

Gardener's Supply: www.gardeners.com
Organic Bouquet: www.organicbouquet.com
Organic Gardening: www.organicgardening.com

GREEN POWER

Energy Star: www.energystar.gov
Environmental Protection Agency Clean Energy: www.epa.gov/cleanenergy
Green Power Options: www.eere.energy.gov/greenpower
Power Scoreboard: www.powerscorecard.org

RECYCLING/SWAPPING

Collective Good: www.collectivegood.com
Craigslist: www.craigslist.org
Earth 911: www.earth911.org
eBay: www.ebay.com
The FreeCycle Network: www.freecycle.org
The National Recycling Coalition: www.nrc-recycle.org

TRAVEL

Green Hotels Association: www.greenhotels.com
Sustainable Travel International: www.sustainabletravelinternational.org
The International Ecotourism Society: www.ecotourism.org

Where it's at...

52 Brilliant Ideas

UNLEASH YOUR CREATIVITY
978-0-399-53325-9

LIVE LONGER
978-0-399-5?

SECRETS OF WINE
978-0-399-53348-8

DETOX YOUR FINANCES
978-0-399-53301-3

CELLULITE SOLUTIONS
978-0-399-53326-6

RAISING A HEALTHY EATER
978-0-399-53339-6

PERIGEE (P) An imprint of Penguin Group (USA)

NEW YORK MILLS PUBLIC LIBRARY
399 Main St.
New York Mills, NY 13417
(315) 736-5391

MEMBER
MID-YORK LIBRARY SYSTEM
Utica, NY 13502